The AN uth League

OHIO SHORT HISTORIES OF AFRICA

This series of Ohio Short Histories of Africa is meant for those who are looking for a brief but lively introduction to a wide range of topics in South African history, politics, and biography, written by some of the leading experts in their fields.

Steve Biko
by Lindy Wilson
ISBN: 978-0-8214-2025-6
e-ISBN: 978-0-8214-4441-2

Spear of the Nation
(Umkhonto weSizwe):
South Africa's Liberation Army,
1960s–1990s
by Janet Cherry
ISBN: 978-0-8214-2026-3
e-ISBN: 978-0-8214-4443-6

Epidemics:
The Story of South Africa's Five
Most Lethal Human Diseases
by Howard Phillips
ISBN: 978-0-8214-2028-7
e-ISBN: 978-0-8214-4442-9

South Africa's Struggle for
Human Rights
by Saul Dubow
ISBN: 978-0-8214-2027-0
e-ISBN: 978-0-8214-4440-5

San Rock Art
by J. D. Lewis-Williams
ISBN: 978-0-8214-2045-4
e-ISBN: 978-0-8214-4458-0

Ingrid Jonker:
Poet under Apartheid
by Louise Viljoen
ISBN: 978-0-8214-2048-5
e-ISBN: 978-0-8214-4460-3

The ANC Youth League
by Clive Glaser
ISBN: 978-0-8214-2044-7
e-ISBN: 978-0-8214-4457-3

Govan Mbeke
by Colin Bundy
ISBN: 978-0-8214-2046-1
e-ISBN: 978-0-8214-4459-7

Contents

Contents

Acknowledgements

I am grateful to Russell Martin for encouraging me to write this book. I would also like to thank Anne Jellema and Andrew Nash for their kindness and intellectual guidance during the preparation of the final manuscript and Julia Jellema-Butler for her assistance with the index. Some of the words and ideas in this book have previously appeared in different form on the pages of Johannesburg's *Business Day* newspaper and I am grateful for permission to reproduce them here.

Anthony Butler
Cape Town
September 2012

1

Introduction

On 8 January 2012 the African National Congress (ANC) celebrated its centenary in Bloemfontein, the city in which it had been founded. By early morning the streets of the city thronged with ANC supporters. When the gates of Free State Stadium were opened, almost 50,000 citizens quickly filled the stands, ready to enjoy a day of food, speech-making and political theatre. For most of those present, the event was a celebration of a remarkable political movement that had survived a century of repression and exile, and emerged as the natural party of post-apartheid government.

ANC leaders in Bloemfontein indulged in more than a moment of self-satisfaction about the capacity of their movement to scale seemingly insuperable obstacles. Three hundred years of white supremacy and segregation culminated, in the second half of the last century, in institutionalised apartheid and the forced relocation of Africans to Bantustans. In the eyes of its champions, the ANC has now begun the long process of remaking this troubled society. It has used its electoral mandate to take unpopular but necessary decisions; it has provided housing, water, sanitation and electricity to millions of citizens; it has created a new system of government out of the disorder of late apartheid; and it has ameliorated the racial and ethnic tensions that are an inevitable consequence of such a tumultuous political history.

As the day drew on in Bloemfontein, and the heat intensified, there were reminders that all has not been well in the liberation movement. Youth League members sang boisterous songs about their leader, Julius Malema, who had not been invited to speak and was shortly to be expelled from the ANC. Workers from the Congress of South African Trade Unions (Cosatu) complained that the celebrations had commenced with a 'centenary golf day' in deference to the sporting preferences of the ANC's new business elite. Mother of the nation Winnie Mandela created a storm all of her own when event organisers failed to reserve a suitable table for her family.

The 'tripartite alliance' between the ANC, Cosatu and the South African Communist Party (SACP) had been fraught with conflict in the run-up to the anniversary. Provinces were exhibiting tendencies towards endemic factionalism and corruption. Such factionalist undercurrents somewhat dissipated the aura of smug satisfaction that might otherwise have persisted during the centenary. The wounds of the 2007 Polokwane conference, at which Thabo Mbeki unsuccessfully stood for a third term as ANC president, had not yet fully healed. Members of a post-Polokwane breakaway party, the Congress of the People (Cope), were conspicuous by their absence from the celebrations; these bitter outcasts were forced to look on as the movement to which they had dedicated their adult lives celebrated its centenary without them.

Looking back on the past century from the vantage point of Bloemfontein, the history of the ANC has been marked by previous episodes of conflict and division. There have been protracted periods in which the very survival of the movement was in doubt. How then has the ANC survived? One secret of its longevity has been its capacity to accommodate changes in its objectives, membership and modes of operation. The chiefs and mission-educated elites who led it during its early years supplemented the movement's ranks later with urban workers, rural activists, organised women and eventually youth. Communist allies brought a 'mass character' to the ANC and changed its modes of protest and organisation. The movement's mostly middle-class leaders ultimately endeavoured to harness the energies of the peri-urban 'masses' that dominated South African politics in the 1980s.

The ANC has also been revitalised fortuitously by powerful socio-economic processes, such as urbanisation and industrialisation, over which it had absolutely no control. And it has been jolted into action by the oppressive political designs of whites. Tactical alliances among European settlers first forced Africans into a struggle for dignity and economic survival; the later social engineering and political repression of segregation and apartheid repeatedly energised black political opposition. Other struggle organisations – notably the Pan Africanist Congress and the offshoots of the black consciousness movement – also created political opportunities that the ANC was able to exploit, belatedly but with often surprising success.

More consistently than its rivals, the ANC has exhibited a capacity for strategic reflection. Its relationship with the SACP helped it intentionally (if sometimes ill-advisedly) to adopt mass and militaristic approaches to political agency, and enabled it to exploit the many advantages of multi-racial organisation. The ANC also waged propaganda war as ruthlessly against fellow struggle movements as against the apartheid regime, and was able to cannibalise or absorb many such rivals.

These factors help to explain the survival of the

liberation movement across decades of anti-apartheid struggle. Since 1994 the ANC has campaigned with great success to replenish its electoral support. Its recruitment drives have taken it to a nominal membership of more than a million. The leadership has dispatched the threat posed by Cope, the first major breakaway the ANC has experienced in half a century, and it has made it difficult for tripartite alliance partners to contemplate a further rupture.

Historians sometimes observe that national–provincial conflicts have been a perennial feature of the ANC and that the movement has been riven with factionalism since at least the 1930s. It would be a mistake, however, to believe that the conflicts within the ANC today merely represent a continuation or resurgence of longstanding and familiar historical divisions. South Africa is undergoing deep processes of class formation that are markedly weakening the internal cohesion of the movement. Much of the ANC leadership is now engaged in the accumulation of wealth on an unprecedented scale; and the interests of the 'empowered' classes are diverging sharply from those of ordinary members. Meanwhile, the black middle class is growing, primarily through access to public sector employment. Such rising classes coexist uneasily with a growing mass membership that remains as poor and economically marginalised as ever.

The ANC possesses three capabilities that allow it to retain a degree of organisational integrity and cohesion. First, it is the party of national government, and it controls eight provincial administrations and the overwhelming majority of municipalities in the country. While the ANC cannot straightforwardly dispense consequent powers of patronage to ensure organisational discipline – patronage has been a force for division almost as much as it has been for unity – the leadership can cement relationships with ordinary people by delivering public services, and it can deliver jobs, tenders and other economic opportunities to its activists.

Second, the ANC continues to possess what its former presidency policy head Joel Netshitenzhe has described as a 'rational centre'. The factions that compete for position in national and provincial conferences are on most occasions not 'hard' or mutually exclusive. There are many activists who are nominated for more than one 'slate' of candidates, and there are many more who will step back from factionalist infighting to insist upon a return to dialogue and compromise. Many of the losers at Polokwane – perhaps the most fraught conference the ANC has ever experienced – were ultimately retained in senior positions. Disagreements over policy and ideology continue to be processed through a seemingly endless internal machinery of dialogue and debate. Although the ANC takes many bad and irrational decisions, it does so through a deliberative process that formally defers to the claims of reason.

Finally, the ANC is united by its ways of telling its own history. When a political movement begins to fragment, it is often consensus about its history that is the first casualty. Competing groups justify their claims for power and advantage on the basis of the alleged injustices or iniquities from the past. The songs that are in evidence at ANC and alliance conferences testify to the presence today of many competing narratives. At the same time, the ANC has been able to sustain and propagate a fairly coherent and consensual grand narrative – albeit one that is increasingly at odds with the interpretations produced by academic historians.

The key dynamics of this quasi-official history can be found frozen in the liberation movement's official logo. Created by the artist and black consciousness activist Thami Mnyele in the early 1980s, this totem continues to possess great appeal for activists and ordinary members. On first observation, it presents a number of unconnected images, drawn at different scales and in diverse colours, crowded together into a rectangular space that can scarcely contain them: a shield, a spear, a wheel, a flag.

The spear and the shield represent the historical

agency of the liberation movement. They summon up a great history stretching from anti-colonial resistance wars to the armed struggle of Umkhonto weSizwe (MK), the joint military wing of the SACP and ANC. They also reflect the movement's continuing 'war' against racial oppression. The fist that holds the spear ostensibly represents the power of a united people; but it also recalls the black consciousness ideology that influenced so many ANC activists in the 1970s.

The wheel symbolises the non- or multi-racialism of the ANC, and more broadly celebrates the movement's unifying character. An earlier version of the logo included a wheel with four spokes, each of which stood for one part of the multi-racial campaigns of the Congress Alliance. The current emblem boasts a wheel with eight spokes, out of deference to the contributions of further 'pillars' of the anti-apartheid struggle such as the trade unions and the United Democratic Front (UDF).

Behind (and sometimes in front of) the wheel there is a horizontal tricolour flag. Its equal bands of black, green and gold represent the oppressed black people of South Africa, the land from which they were displaced, and the mineral wealth that lies under the ground. Together these colours symbolise the elements of historical oppression and dispossession from which the ANC promises liberation.

Official histories

The expected highlight of the ANC's centenary day celebration in Bloemfontein was President Jacob Zuma's late-afternoon delivery of the 'January 8th Statement'. During the decades of ANC exile, this annual communiqué was awaited with excitement by ANC sympathisers and underground activists. By tradition it set out the strategic analysis of the ANC's national executive committee (NEC) and detailed the priorities that would guide ANC activities in the year ahead.

The centenary year's January 8th statement was considered sufficiently important to be printed as a booklet for distribution to branches.[1] When President Zuma delivered a condensed version of the statement to the stadium audience, his delivery was laboured and monotonous. (Zuma, as so often seemingly unfamiliar with the contents of the speech he was reading, had apparently partied late into the night at a gala celebration.) Thousands of disappointed activists fled the heat of the stadium long before the two-hour oration had concluded. Those who remained were treated to a prolonged meditation on the history of the ANC.

Although the ANC's centenary had encouraged an outpouring of reflection on the history of the movement, no consensus had emerged about how such a history should be written. In truth, historians are not disinterested chroniclers of distant events. The questions they ask are motivated by their preoccupations today and by their fears and hopes for tomorrow. Most historians have characterised the ANC, with more or less sympathy, as an organisation of African elites in the decade of its formation; as a somewhat moribund historical bystander in the 1920s and 1930s; as an increasingly radical actor in the struggle for political rights and justice in the 1940s; as the mobilising force behind a campaign of defiance in the 1950s; as an exiled or imprisoned liberation movement in the 1960s and 1970s; as a catalyst for armed struggle from the 1960s to the 1980s; as a mass party in the early 1990s; and, finally, as a troubled party of government after 1994.

The movement that historians describe has changed dramatically across its history. In the second decade of the twentieth century, the ANC was led by missionary-educated professionals and ruling chiefs and it was driven by a thirst for rights – but also for land. The ANC that launched the defiance campaigns of the 1950s, by contrast, was preoccupied with the politics of the urban masses in the burgeoning cities of South Africa. The small band of exiles that languished in Lusaka in the early 1970s shared little with the

Jacob Zuma at a meeting of the ANC National General Council, Durban, 2010. (Rogan Ward)

dynamic mass movement that propelled political negotiations to their conclusion in the early 1990s.

Less sympathetic writers have sometimes painted a dark portrait of the historical ANC. For some of its critics, it has been a communist puppet, a dinosaur or a political parasite that has betrayed the poor South Africans it once promised to liberate. Sceptics claim that the ANC's recent achievements – bringing political stability, creating a credible programme of government, and neutralising social conflict – have been self-serving or transitory. They insist that the ANC has wasted the opportunities presented by a global economic boom and that its greed and unforgivable policy errors have left millions languishing in poverty.

Over the past decade South Africans have indeed endured deep inequality and unemployment, an AIDS crisis, and deepening corruption. Policy blunders resulted in the humiliation of rolling national power blackouts. Devastating 'xenophobic violence', much of it directed against citizens from the north of the country, exploded in 2008. Community 'service delivery' protests have become commonplace, and in some communities a return to the relentless civil conflict of the late apartheid years now seems conceivable. Inside the ANC there have been episodes of open rebellion against the leadership, and debilitating battles for succession to the movement's presidency and other senior offices have become routine.

When explaining the current travails of the movement, ANC leaders sometimes turn to history. Their preoccupation with the past is not merely a form of escapism. It is upon claims about the past that assertions of legitimate power today depend. President Jacob Zuma's January 8th statement in Bloemfontein was an expression of a new and increasingly bold narrative that explains the ANC's unique historical character and its consequent entitlement to rule.

This is not the first time that sympathetic writers have presented the ANC's victory in the struggle against apartheid as ordained by history. Even non-partisan professional historians tend to view history from the victors' perspective. Events and actions are all too easily allocated places in a wider narrative that culminates in ANC victory. Partisan historians are, however, now more inclined than ever to treat the ANC's post-apartheid ascendancy as pre-ordained. Their official narrative interprets the movement's periods of passivity, and even its major blunders, as opportunities for political regeneration and strategic learning. While the great liberation movement occasionally trips over its own feet, it quickly rights itself and resumes its inexorable progress towards its meeting with destiny.

The official history presented in Bloemfontein

incorporates a selective recording of events. It catalogues turning points and internal strategic decisions that allegedly brought the cause of national freedom closer. This narrative, as we shall see, tends to erase the movement's political rivals from history. It also presents the ANC as a privileged instrument of historical destiny, as the only legitimate champion of the people's freedom and as the unique custodian of South Africans' hopes for the future. Historically innocent Youth League activists have been taught to believe that history is on their movement's side.

What exactly is this thing called the ANC? The movement's intellectuals discern within the ANC's complex past an historical identity – a set of essential features that make the movement recognisably itself across the hundred years of its existence. The organisation has, moreover, always been constituted in part by how its supporters have conceived of it. ANC activists therefore shoulder an obligation to understand their movement's historical identity and to ensure that it is reproduced into the future. For such intellectuals, the ANC is more than just an organisation: it is also an idea.

The current quasi-official histories of the ANC incorporate three interrelated notions that help to explain the movement's historical endurance and accomplishments: a conception of power or agency;

a notion of unity; and an understanding of human liberation. This book explores how these contested ideas have shaped the ANC in the past, and it speculates about how they may inform its leaders' choices in the future. Along the way, the book will try to explain how and why the ANC has survived, and what, if anything, might be the purposes of its continued existence.

2

Agency

Perhaps the most fundamental distinction we can draw lies between that which merely happens and that which is done. One way to conceive of the history of the ANC is as a search for the capacity to act in a world of largely incomprehensible and seemingly inexorable economic and social upheavals.

The South African Native National Congress (SANNC), later renamed the African National Congress, was formed in 1912 by a tiny elite of African chiefs and Christian educated professionals. These founders were determined to assert themselves against the recent creation of a white supremacist state, the Union of South Africa; but they were also the survivors of centuries of social turmoil that originated in the imperial project and, later, in capitalist accumulation. Such leaders struggled to conceptualise realistic objectives and then to identify strategies and instruments with which to achieve them. They were obliged to act in an environment they could not begin to control, and their early instruments of political assertion proved almost totally ineffectual.

Looking backwards, the establishment of permanent Dutch settlement in the 17th century had begun with the destruction of the hunting and herding societies of the Cape. Peoples known today as Khoikhoi or Khoisan, present in the south-west of the continent since around 1000 BC, were devastated by disease and violence in the early period of Dutch East India Company rule. In contrast, the major African political kingdoms of the subcontinent proved to be more robust. These hereditary chiefdoms had expanded into what is today South Africa from around the third century AD. By the time of European settlement they had almost reached the west of South Africa. Their resilience in the face of European conquest would later be reflected in their widespread distribution two centuries after the arrival of white settlers.

Farmers of Dutch descent drifted eastward from the original settlement at Cape Town in search of grazing land. By the middle of the 18th century they had become involved in sporadic conflicts with the Xhosa people. Frontier wars marked the next hundred years and did not conclude until the second half of the 19th century. In these conflicts the settlers' advantages, such as their ability to exploit divisions in African society, the technological superiority of their firearms, and their ability to store wealth in their more sophisticated economic system, failed to confer overwhelming superiority. As a result, the political settlement reached at the Cape under what had by then become British rule included civil rights and the vote for African property-owning men.

Conflicts associated with a centralisation of the Zulu kingdom in the 1820s had meanwhile dislocated African societies across the interior. At around the same time, Boers driven out of a now inhospitable British-run Cape Colony undertook a series of episodic migrations (later celebrated as the 'Great Trek') that deposited white settlements across the 'highveld' to the north, soon to be organised under the republics of the Orange Free State and the Transvaal. Though the Boers were vulnerable and widely dispersed, by 1870 they had established a presence across wide tracts of the African interior that they would later be unwilling to relinquish.

Despite the robustness of African societies in the face of settler competition, they were confronted by a combination of blunt coercion and pernicious legal and institutional constraints, in the Boer republics above all. Starting in the Cape, large-scale Christian conversions from the 1860s, and the rise of an African petty bourgeoisie, marked the growing incorporation of native elites into the intellectual and commercial life of a global empire.

After 1870 the settler and indigenous populations were swept along in a fresh tide of impersonal forces. Diamonds were discovered in 1867, attracting foreign investment and initiating modern capitalism in South Africa. After 1886, the focus of investment and development switched to the newly discovered goldfields of the Witwatersrand. The extraordinary social upheavals of industrialisation and urbanisation that affected both black and white were accompanied by legal and institutional innovations designed to drive Africans into the labour force. What is more, the imperial power began for the first time to engage seriously with the development of the once-sleepy subcontinent. In order to provide the necessary political framework, it set out to impose control over the entire region, first by breaking native and Boer resistance. The Xhosa were decisively defeated in 1878 and Zulu resistance was later crushed at Ulundi. The British went on to subdue the Pedi people, and then to break down the defiance of the Boers in the South African or Anglo-Boer War of 1899–1902. The end of African resistance was signalled by the putting down of Bambatha's rebellion in Natal in 1906.

The inauguration of the Union of South Africa in 1910 from a motley collection of colonies and African

Rural protests against forced removals, Cornfields, Natal, 1988.
(Gille de Vlieg)

chiefdoms marked the culmination of a comprehensive process of state creation. The British-sponsored state could now enforce contracts, regulate labour, levy taxes, and ensure strategic security across South Africa. By so doing it could ensure that the mineral wealth of South Africa would be exploited by British conglomerates. Union entrenched the privileges of whites over other races by giving them a virtual monopoly of political power (although propertied African males were still entitled to vote in the Cape).

ANC intellectuals sometimes place such crushing disempowerment in the context of a wider deterioration in the political circumstances of black peoples around the world. In 1884, the leading European powers carved up Africa among themselves. Soon thereafter the circumstances of former African slaves deteriorated across the Americas. 'As a race', the latest ANC official narrative observes, 'virtually all Africans had been reduced to a subject people, ruled and governed by others, usually whites from Europe or their descendants naturalized in other climes'.[2]

Dispossession

The SANNC was formed by an African elite that felt both betrayed and threatened by the Act of Union. In many respects, the ANC's founders were typical products of British rule. As Moeletsi Mbeki observes, African nationalism was 'a movement of the small, Westernised black elite that emerged under colonialism. Its fight was always for inclusion in the colonial system so that it, too, could benefit from the spoils of colonialism.'[3] Some of the ANC's early leaders were chiefs and kings. Others were members of an African professional class – lawyers, teachers, doctors, churchmen – that had been educated in mission schools and sometimes in British and American universities. They had internalised the central values of the colonised native middle class across the Empire and they avowedly pursued freedom, civilisation, respectability and progress.

They were primarily coverts to optimistic Protestant faiths that anticipated the return of Christ after a thousand years. During this millennium of peace, virtuous believers were enjoined to engage in wholesome acts of social development. Mission schools and colleges such as Healdtown (Methodist), Lovedale (United Free Church of Scotland), the University College of Fort Hare (Methodist, Presbyterian and Anglican) and St Peter's (Anglican) therefore propagated 'post-Millennial' variants of Protestantism that encouraged evangelism, temperance and the celebration of commerce as an avenue for civilisation. Such a religion taught its new adherents that progress towards a more equal social order was a matter of divine inevitability rather than of political struggle, and it meanwhile imparted a veneer of moral seriousness to the Empire.[4]

In the wider society, a different 'pre-Millennial' brand of Christianity, propagated by fundamentalist and Pentecostal churches, began to evangelise from the 1890s. The converts of such churches viewed the world as irredeemably corrupt and eagerly anticipated the Kingdom of God, which would come about suddenly and at any moment – and only after the destruction of all existing social orders through a cataclysmic conflict that would culminate in Armageddon. For such believers, change in human affairs came about from outside history and participation in politics was a dangerous distraction from the work of purifying the soul. Such beliefs would later map onto the insurrectionist ideologies propagated by the proponents of political revolution.

Whether post-Millennial or pre-Millennial, all Christian converts typically believed that secular government is given by God and that believers must consequently respect the authority of the state. The office of governor is divinely ordained and the sword is reserved to those who rule. As the Letter to the Romans, chapter 13, instructs, 'Let every soul be subject unto the higher powers. For there is no power but of God: the powers that be are ordained of God … Render therefore to all their dues: tribute to whom tribute [is due]; custom to whom custom; fear to whom fear; honour to whom honour.'

Christian converts were, however, to some degree pulled between the expectations and demands of the colonial power, the Christian religion and traditional society.[5] Even the most sanguine members of the African elite that assembled in Bloemfontein on 8 January 1912 recognised that the Empire was no longer a reliable protector of their rights and aspirations. Political freedoms and the dignity of the male franchise were under threat of being stripped away and Africans were being driven from the land. The first decade of the century had seen concerted efforts by chiefs and other members of the African elite to acquire land commercially, and this aspiration would persist in the decades ahead. But in 1913, soon after the formation of the SANNC, the Natives Land Act allocated 87 per cent of land to whites and began to close down native land purchases and non-labour-based tenancies.

The SANNC's leaders responded as best they could by exhausting the meagre political instruments available to them. They called public meetings and tried to sway opinion in London, most famously by means of a 1914 petition to protest against the Land Act and a 1919 delegation to ask for the political rights of Africans to be respected. Soon, however, the settler state further circumscribed Africans' opportunities and freedoms.

Freedom of movement was checked by systematic labour controls that were progressively tightened. Annual migrant labour cycles had begun on the sugar fields of Natal. Later, migrancy became a more general domestic and subcontinental cheap labour system, feeding the country's mining, commercial and agricultural sectors. The 1923 Natives (Urban Areas) Act created legal tools to entrench further the practices of 'influx control' by means of 'pass laws'. Initially a partly discretionary process to earn some cash income, influx control quickly became unavoidable for Africans as taxes, dispossession and population growth squeezed rural populations and pushed them out to the towns and cities. From the Witwatersrand, the Chamber of Mines developed a network of chiefs, traders and criminals to recruit young, male workers for the gold mines. By 1920, a centralised labour migration system managed more than 200,000 workers.

The ANC faltered during the hard economic times of the 1920s. The black petty bourgeoisie was undergoing a crisis of religious identity as the promise of inevitable social progress was contradicted by relentless experiences of injustice and racism. Intellectuals began to revisit their African heritages and identities. The ANC's rivals, such as rural trade unions and the urban Communist Party of South Africa (CPSA), began to outstrip it. Though the CPSA had fewer than 2000 members by 1928, the Party was both active and non-racial.[6] On the instructions of the Communist International, the CPSA adopted as its central objective the achievement of an independent native republic as a precursor to a workers' and peasants' republic and an eventual socialist revolution. Although communist ideas had some influence within the ANC, the movement languished under a defensive and confused Christian leadership.

The ANC could easily have died in the 1930s. However, between 1933 and 1948 South Africa emerged into a second industrial revolution on the back of a rise in the gold price and increased demand for manufactured exports as the North prepared for war. The wartime economic bonanza after 1939 brought unprecedented African urbanisation. Black trade unions blossomed, higher-skilled jobs were opened to Africans, and colour bars in many sectors were raised.

The CPSA organised anti-pass campaigns, and bus boycotts became a major instrument of black protest. Strikes, land invasions, stayaways and localised riots occurred with greater frequency on the Rand. However, the ANC was not a force in organising this swelling tide of resistance. In 1943, under what remained an

Anti-pass march, Pretoria, 1955. (Drum, *1955*)

elite leadership, the movement published its 'African Claims' document. This did mark a change in the objectives of ANC political struggle in that it included demands for self-government and for political rights for Africans. However, its intention was to recruit African graduates to bolster the membership of the organisation. The following year the ANC failed to support the Alexandra bus boycott.

If international economic conditions and industrialisation were the key driving forces behind this period of African political mobilisation, it took intensified racism to precipitate a coherent political response from the ANC. As a result of post-war efforts to turn back the effects of African urbanisation, whites began to formulate increasingly aggressive segregationist controls. This engendered co-operation between Africans, Coloureds and Indians, and in 1947 the ANC and the Indian Congress signed the so-called Doctors' Pact. At the same time, a younger generation of activists, including Nelson Mandela and Oliver Tambo, galvanised the Congress Youth League (CYL) into action.

The CYL pulled off a remarkable putsch at the ANC's December conference in 1949, replacing ANC president A.B. Xuma with J.S. Moroka, securing almost half of the executive seats, and elevating Walter Sisulu to the office of secretary-general. The

CYL also drew up a Programme of Action, calling for the adoption of techniques such as strikes, stayaways and boycotts, which had been pioneered by rival organisations, including the CPSA. As the historian Saul Dubow observes, 'For the first time in its history the organisation was able to plan, lead and execute a systematic national campaign of political action.'[7]

Between 1950 and 1952, the ascendant radicals then achieved an unexpected rapprochement with the communist and non-African activists they had earlier mistrusted. Impressed by the mass actions of the CPSA, and by the Party's African leaders, they imported mass mobilisation techniques, pioneered originally by Indian communists, into the ANC.[8] Youth League leaders were among the leading intellectuals of the ANC of their time. And the Marxism they initially disparaged unexpectedly helped many of them to make some sense of the bewildering second industrial revolution on the Rand, which had fundamentally reshaped social and political life in its wake.

Launched in 1952, the Defiance Campaign helped generate mass resistance to freshly passed apartheid laws. 'Defiance' was a rhetorical escalation in that it took the ANC beyond the idea of 'passive resistance', which had framed its actions in the 1940s. It was nevertheless still defensive in that violence was shunned and the costs of defiance were borne by

31

the defiant themselves. The variety of anti-regime protests meanwhile widened. Women mobilised on a significant scale for the first time around pass laws and bans on home brewing of beer. The local dimension of politics, dominated by women and hitherto largely ignored by male ANC leaders, became more central to the movement's activity. In rural areas, local struggles were under way (albeit in this case largely unnoticed by the ANC leadership) and these would later burst out, above all in the Pondoland and Sekhukhuneland revolts of the late 1950s.

During the 1950s the character of the demands made by the ANC changed as housing, employment, education and self-government all became central to protest. Such demands were drawn together into the Freedom Charter, which was adopted at the Congress of the People at Kliptown in 1955. This document famously stated that 'South Africa belongs to all who live in it, black and white'. It incorporated demands for the nationalisation of mineral wealth, banks and monopoly capital. The signatories exhibited a conscious and deliberate multi-racialism, albeit one that echoed the state's own racial definitions.

Sharpeville and Soweto

Under the auspices of the National Party, which came to power in 1948, Afrikaner intellectuals developed ambitious plans to widen the scope of apartheid in the late 1950s: segregationist doctrine was to be supplanted by the more dangerous notion of 'separate development'. Segregation had involved an explicit racial hierarchy in legislative and political practice. Separate development, by contrast, would rest on alleged equality between ethnic groups, inspired in part by decolonisation elsewhere in Africa. Africans' political rights were to be transferred into ten or so Bantustans. Mass forced removals of 'incorrectly' located black people, deliberate 'retribalisation' of African people and newly created homelands or Bantustans, to which they were removed, would soon result in an unprecedented period of social engineering.

In 1960, however, when such plans were on the verge of implementation, South African politics were dramatically changed – and, once again, the intervening force came from outside the ANC. Within the movement 'Africanists' had opposed the Freedom Charter because of its accommodation of whites and its partial embrace of communist ideas and partners. In 1959, many younger activists, under the charismatic leadership of Robert Sobukwe, broke away to form the Pan Africanist Congress (PAC).

Congress of the People, Kliptown, Soweto, 1955. (Museum Africa)

© Museum Africa / Africa Media Online

Immediately a rival to the ANC, and keen to trump it, the PAC launched its anti-pass campaign ahead of the ANC's on 21 March 1960. On that day, the police opened fire on a peaceful crowd of protesters at Sharpeville, to the south of Johannesburg, killing 69 and wounding 186. The government declared a state of emergency, banned the PAC and the ANC, and arrested more than 10,000 activists from both parties, as well as from left-wing and liberal organisations. Early white panic brought calls for political reform, capital flight, white emigration and the temporary suspension of the pass laws. Within a year, however, the National Party achieved a stunning electoral success. Investment, including foreign investment, returned and, with it, rapid economic growth. Europeans began to migrate to South Africa in record numbers. And government increased spending on repression, the police and the military, and intensified the system of urban influx control.[9]

Ultimately, it may have been the anti-apartheid struggle that suffered the most sustained losses from Sharpeville. The PAC began a period of debilitating exile. Leaders from the ANC and the renamed and now illegal South African Communist Party (SACP) decided that the era of non-violent resistance was over. This decision had already been in the making for some years: a number of communist activists had been lobbying for this change and they had already consulted with international allies in China and the Soviet Union. Sharpeville made the turn to violence inescapable, a decision that was to bring important and, in many respects, negative consequences for the struggle against apartheid. As the ANC explained in a manifesto for MK's launch, armed struggle had become necessary because government had removed all space for non-violent political protest, imposing 'virtual martial law' and crushing a proposed general strike. 'The choice is not ours', the ANC's flyer observed; 'it has been made by the Nationalist government.'

MK henceforth drained the ANC of its leaders, diverted its energies into the building of a parallel organisation, and reduced engagement with the urban masses. Politics became a spectacle – something that the ANC did on behalf of the people – rather than a process in which the people would be engaged.[10] Violence became central to the symbolism and ethos of the movement.

Such tendencies were exacerbated by the destruction of whatever domestic ANC organisation was left after its banning in 1960. The Rivonia arrests of 1963 exposed the amateurishness of the leadership and culminated in the Rivonia trial of 1964. For an ANC that had become accustomed to mass rallies, 'secrecy was not something that came easily'.[11] After

Sharpeville funeral, 1960. (Peter Magubane)

Rivonia, the ANC virtually ceased to exist for a decade. Nelson Mandela, Walter Sisulu and Govan Mbeki were locked up on Robben Island. Oliver Tambo was forced into desperate exile. The underground was infiltrated and placed under relentless surveillance.[12]

In the event, armed struggle turned out to be almost impossible to prosecute. South Africa had a flat terrain and border regions policed by tightly organised and heavily armed white farmers. Neighbouring states could not, or would not, serve as secure rear bases for ANC fighters. The implications of these weaknesses became clear in 1967, when MK began a joint campaign with the Zimbabwe African Political Union (Zapu) liberation movement in Rhodesia. Seeking a route into South Africa from Zambia through Rhodesia's Wankie game reserve, two groups totalling around 50 fighters were routed. The SACP fancifully heralded the Wankie campaign as the 'start of the South African revolution' and predicted that guerrillas would 'spread south of the Limpopo in an ever-rising tide of mass revolution'.[13] In truth, dozens of fighters died, and the rest retreated in disarray to Botswana, where they were arrested. The Sipolilo campaign launched from eastern Zambia at the end of 1967 suffered even heavier casualties. At this stage, not a single shot had been fired by MK freedom fighters on South African soil.

In early 1969, the charismatic MK leader Chris Hani

wrote what was to become a famous memorandum of complaint against the ANC leadership. He described 'a machinery which is an end unto itself', an 'overconcentration of people in offices' and the replacement of revolutionaries with 'globetrotting' professional politicians. Hani also lambasted nepotism, 'mysterious business enterprises', and the ANC's security department's involvement in 'secret trials and secret executions'.[14]

In a meeting held at Morogoro, Tanzania, in 1969 in response to such discontent, the ANC fatefully locked itself into a continuation of its armed struggle – although it recognised that such a struggle required a complementary political engagement through an internal ANC underground. Military struggle had become a propaganda instrument that was used to differentiate the ANC from its rivals. The SACP was the dominant force in MK and, through it, became the dominant force within a quasi-militarised ANC.

The movement moved into survivalist mode; in the early 1970s, it comprised perhaps 130 people in Lusaka, 250 activists in Tanzania, 100 in Botswana, Lesotho and Swaziland combined, and perhaps 20 students in Soviet universities. These were the years of what the SACP leader Joe Slovo called the 'diseases of exile': ethnic factionalism, corruption and a lack of political direction. In such settings as Lusaka, where the ANC was headquartered, comrades developed a 'culture of not rocking the boat, of not wanting to confront each other'.[15] This resulted in deep-seated problems being veiled and in errant behaviour being accommodated rather than rooted out. These were almost equally dark years on Robben Island. The one bright light was Oliver Tambo's patient success in building a powerful international diplomatic presence for the ANC.

Some historians claim that the underground inside South Africa at least was not as moribund as it appeared.[16] The ANC lived on in political culture, with the names and deeds of the ANC leaders of the 1950s passed from parent to child. Congress symbols endured; released political prisoners provided a constantly refilled reservoir of ANC memories; and there were episodes of ANC leaflet distribution and sporadic propaganda successes. Yet the conventional wisdom that, after 1960, the ANC was largely dormant within the country, and ineffectual in exile, nevertheless remains broadly persuasive.

Again the ANC might have died, and again salvation came from outside. Black trade unions within South Africa began to flex their newly formed shop-floor muscle. Then a new generation of political activists, energised by the independence of former Portuguese colonies in the early and mid-1970s, campaigned against the apartheid state under the influence of

42

liberation theology and black consciousness (BC) ideas. BC emerged quite independently of the ANC; and in the early 1970s, exile ANC leaders became preoccupied with the danger that it might become more than just a rival to the liberation movement.

The watershed youth revolt that began in Soweto on 16 June 1976 shook investor confidence in South Africa in a more lasting way than Sharpeville. It also astonished ANC leaders in exile and in prison. Soweto resulted in an exodus of young people into exile where they swelled the ranks of the languishing ANC (which, however, was not languishing so much as to be unable to accommodate and incorporate them successfully).

Despite early uneasiness and even repudiation of the actions of the youth, senior exile leaders, including Oliver Tambo and Alfred Nzo, soon kicked off strenuous and sustained efforts to appropriate the spirit and accomplishments of the Soweto uprising.[17] In an interview more than a decade later, Jacob Zuma still claimed that the black consciousness movement had been infiltrated by the ANC and that MK actions were responsible for 'the spirit of resistance' that drove the Soweto uprising.[18] MK rocket and limpet mine attacks on electricity and energy infrastructure and army bases in the late 1970s conceivably did have hidden political repercussions. The regime maintained power by terror; and MK's attacks freed some of the

43

Workers satirise leaders of the apartheid regime and Bantustans, Cosatu cultural day, 1985. (Santu Mofokeng)

people from fear.[19] Armed actions, however, reduced the regime's willingness to contemplate change, gave substance to claims that the ANC was a terrorist organisation, and bolstered the National Party's 'anti-communist' credentials at home and abroad.

Transitions

The ANC continued to be committed to a multi-faceted approach to the struggle with what were known as the 'four pillars': armed operations, mass mobilisation, underground organisation and international solidarity. Although ANC leaders found it impossible to pursue domestic organisation directly, the movement was able to infiltrate and indirectly influence many of the vehicles for resistance and change that did emerge.

Pretoria was progressively deprived of buffer regimes to the north after the independence of Angola, Mozambique and Zimbabwe was secured. The Soviet Union's debilitation brought the proxy Cold War in Africa to a close. Economic crisis and international illegitimacy pushed the ANC and the National Party (NP) towards negotiation, though organised political opposition was necessary to close down the NP's avenues for delay. The most important single organisation in this multi-faceted struggle was the ANC. It played an important (but not determining) role in the 1983 formation of the United Democratic

MK parade, Soweto, 1990. (Paul Weinberg)

Front (UDF), which brought together civic, religious, student and labour bodies on a common platform of anti-apartheid struggle. Independent black trade unions in the 1980s formed a formidable ANC-aligned Federation (later Congress) of South African Trade Unions (Cosatu).

What ultimately rendered apartheid unsustainable was individual acts in defiance of influx control, repeated by millions of workers. Between 1960 and 1970, while the African population in white urban areas fell by over 200,000 through forced removals, the population of the Bantustans grew by almost a million. The extreme overcrowding and impoverishment that resulted in the reserves, and the artificial reduction in available labour in the white urban areas, created a strong incentive for workers to defy controls.

Direct ANC influence was negligible when it came to the decisive wave of local insurrections that began in the Vaal Triangle (today, Gauteng province) in 1984 and later spread to Natal, the Eastern Cape, and Free State. Rebels primarily targeted collaborators and corrupt local councillors. As Dubow observes, 'even if it wanted to claim credit for the unrest, the ANC was not the orchestrator of a revolt'.[20] Moreover, the exile leaders' attempt to capitalise on these localised uprisings was tactically inept. The dominant view among the leadership was that township defence committees could be transformed into 'combat groups' that would challenge the apartheid regime. As a result of this miscalculation, MK infiltrated 150 poorly equipped and undertrained cadres in 1985–6. This effort briefly doubled MK presence on the ground before the capture and death of these soldiers at the hands of police and state security services.

At the ANC's consultative conference in Kabwe, Zambia, in June 1985, the leadership could not abandon quasi-revolutionary doctrines that closed down potential avenues for political engagement. Part of the reason for this is that Marxist theory of revolution is dogged by troubling paradoxes of agency. Revolution is driven by fundamental economic forces rather than by political choices. If revolution is truly inevitable, however, there does not seem to be any reason for revolutionaries to actually bring it about.[21] Leninist doctrines, moreover, added an additional dimension of anti-democratic distance to the activities of party leaders. The ANC elite enjoined MK fighters and local community activists to unleash violence on the apartheid state. But ANC strategists took upon themselves the secretive responsibility for discerning which appropriate operational strategies might be available to realise whatever potential for revolution might be present in any particular historical conjuncture.

When O.R. Tambo told South Africans to render the country 'ungovernable' in 1985, he was trying to place the ANC at the head of an unfolding social revolution. The inability of the ANC either to instigate or to control violence became clear when international uproar greeted the practice of 'necklacing'. Far from being a potential instigator of such attacks, the ANC was a distant observer. In September 1986, the ANC secretary-general Alfred Nzo, in an interview with the London *Times*, captured the exile leaders' detachment perfectly: 'Whatever the people decide to use to eliminate those enemy elements is their decision. If they decide to use necklacings, we support it.'

In its early years, the ANC had been subservient to the civilising project of Empire. In the decades of inertia that followed, the ANC's Christian leaders eschewed anti-regime mass protest in anticipation of divine extra-historical intervention. While the tradition of Christian rights-based liberalism that emerged would later help the ANC to frame a balanced post-apartheid constitution, it proved debilitating in the struggle against institutionalised racism.

Equally debilitating was that the post-1960 ANC leadership internalised a quasi-Marxist conception of inexorable change. The central responsibility of the ANC leaders became one of seizing the opportunities presented to them by history. Although the ANC's advocacy of a military struggle delivered propaganda gains to the movement, it did so at the cost of slowing political transition.[22]

The militaristic tenor of the decades of exile has also infected present-day political rhetoric and symbolism. An older generation of ANC activists took intellectuals' assertions about strategy and tactics with a pinch of salt. Many of them were able to inspect the merits of different systems of government – including failing communist states and largely admirable social democracies – at first hand. New generations of ANC activists, on the other hand, have had less exposure to the practical lessons of history. They are sometimes inclined to take the Leninist slogans and militaristic posturing of the past at face value and to reproduce them in their own political actions. For this reason, meetings of ANC youth organisations are increasingly dominated by political theatre, militarism and machismo.

Youth League struggle songs continue to glorify violence; and a gratuitous militarism sometimes afflicts even elderly ANC cadres. In a recent speech setting out her priorities as incoming African Union Commission chairperson, for example, Nkosazana Dlamini-Zuma celebrated the 'great African armies in Isandhlwana in South Africa and Sudan' that 'defeated the mighty armies of the British Empire'. The

Duduza protesters, 1986. (Paul Weinberg)

militaristic celebration of warrior kings and prophets is not a major asset when confronting the developmental challenges of the decades ahead. Presumptions of historical inevitability, punctuated by militaristic assertiveness, are unlikely to become conducive to effective government at any point in the 21st century.

State agency

In the past ANC leaders were understandably preoccupied with the seizure, or negotiated capture, of state power, rather than with the exercise of the power of the state. Marxist state theory has in any event focused primarily on the functions that the state serves in a given historical epoch or 'mode of production'. The state in the capitalist mode of production is precisely a capitalist state: it performs the function of facilitating the accumulation of capital by the bourgeoisie; it coordinates the exploitation of the working class; and it protects the appropriating class against the poor, if necessary by using the iron fist of state coercion to subdue them. In more subtle formulations, it promotes the legitimacy of an unjust social order as well as advancing the accumulation and concentration of wealth.

Such a dramatically negative conception of the state was understandably appealing to activists in the era of high apartheid: indeed, the South African state was almost a caricature of the sinister capitalist state. What is more, after the banning of the CPSA and the ANC, communist theoreticians were increasingly preoccupied by the experiences of post-colonial societies elsewhere in Africa. They developed a sceptical interpretation of the parasitical relationship that appeared to emerge between post-colonial elites and an entrenched neo-colonialist state.

Many ANC exiles had extended personal exposure to more benign variants of the 'capitalist state': in the Netherlands, Scandinavia and the UK. What was missing from the ANC's development in the post-banning decades, however, was any extended intellectual engagement with the social democratic and democratic socialist traditions. Post-war social democracy emerged out of a protracted struggle to humanise the operations of the capitalist economic system, primarily through the adoption of bourgeois political practices and the modification of capitalist economic institutions. In the 1930s, the struggle for 'parliamentary socialism' appeared to have been in vain; but in the post-war decades, a state fortified by wartime planning and state-centred economic theory suddenly became a powerful agency of social transformation.

Across a range of European countries, leftist parties came to power determined to improve the lives of workers and the poor. They progressively extended the reach of the state through corporatist, planning and welfare state interventions. They experimented with nationalisation, new forms of collectivism and worker participation, and the development of inter-state cooperation to mitigate the hazards created by international trade and capital flows.

The successes of European social democracy posed a major challenge to the dogmas of Soviet Marxism. They also exposed the limitations of the evasive state theories developed within post-war Western Marxism. All the same, the CPSA, and later the SACP, joined the shrinking band of declining European communist parties that castigated social democracy as a futile reformism. When the ANC secured political power in 1994, it brought with it an antipathy not merely to the capitalist economy through which it would have to work, but also a hostility to the very 'capitalist state' itself. This has made it difficult for the ANC to realise what are, in content, mostly social democratic objectives and aspirations.

Since 1994, the ANC has used political power to make available water, sanitation, electricity, schools, houses and clinics – basic public services that were previously a near-preserve of whites. The improvements in quality of life that have often resulted cannot be overemphasised. But now that the low fruits of post-apartheid service delivery have been picked, underlying anti-capitalist and anti-statist sentiments are resurfacing, supplanted at times of crisis by a restless militancy. What is missing above all from ANC conceptions of government is a sense of how the state can be used to harness the dynamic energies of a capitalist economy and to mitigate the inequality and alienation that such an economy is predisposed to generate.

Liberation movement intellectuals have meanwhile used their quasi-Marxist doctrines to subtract chance, complexity and human weakness from history, cloaking the ANC in an extra-constitutional mantle of unquestionable political authority and validating their own claims to serve as the instruments of historical destiny. A philosophy dominated by historical inevitability, in which the scientific knowledge of the Party is the key to understanding human affairs, can have a profoundly undemocratic influence on political leaders.

3

Unity

In a reflective speech delivered in the ANC's anniversary year, the organisation's deputy president, Kgalema Motlanthe, observed that 'in the ANC nothing matters more than unity'. The movement, he noted, was 'founded on the principle of unity, the unity of the people. And it is that principle which we must take to heart; it is that principle which sustained the ANC throughout these glorious 100 years.'[23] But there is a conundrum at the heart of such claims. ANC leaders insist that their movement stands, above all other things, for unity. But, at the same time, the ANC has been variously and deeply divided across its history; and it is today more starkly factionalised and conflict-ridden than ever.

The ANC's commitment to unity has been interpreted in diverse ways over the century of the movement's existence. The early leaders of the ANC were preoccupied with 'tribal' or ethnic divisions between African peoples. In later decades, the movement's elites turned their attention to expressions of racial, ideological, gendered and generational disharmony. The pursuit of unity has been celebrated as a major strength of the ANC and it has at times brought significant political benefits to the movement and to the society. But certain hazards have also flowed from this aspect of the ANC's avowed historical mission. Differences have been suppressed or concealed rather than confronted; tensions have developed between different substantive concepts of unity; and the mutation of unity into enforced oneness has on occasion posed challenges to party democracy and to the entrenchment of constitutional democracy.

Tribalism

The first paradox of unity in the history of the ANC concerns the circumstances of the movement's creation: unity was the product of enforced division. The notable Africans who gathered together in Bloemfontein in January 1912 to create the South African Native National Congress (SANNC) were confronted with a new kind of antagonist: an emergent white supremacist state. It was the sharp division between white and black that the Act of Union threatened to entrench that made a project of African unification suddenly essential.

The delegates to that foundational congress came not only from South Africa but also from Zambia, Botswana, Lesotho and Swaziland. Although many of the organisers and intellectuals of the nascent organisation were educated Christian professionals, the founders included local chiefs and kings and the rulers of African kingdoms in Lesotho, Botswana and Swaziland. The significance that the African elite attributed to the need for unity is plain from the much-quoted words of Pixley ka Isaka Seme, soon to be treasurer of the new organisation, in a paper on 'native union' which he delivered three months in advance of the movement's foundation. He insisted that Africans must learn lessons from their history of discord. Africans across the region, he insisted, had been the victims of divide and rule strategies of the part of the colonial authorities. Seme denounced the 'demon of racialism, the aberrations of the Xosa–Fingo feud, the animosity that exists between the Zulus and the Tongaas, between the Basutos and every other Native'. This animosity 'must be buried and forgotten; it has shed among us sufficient blood! We are one people. These divisions, these jealousies, are the cause of all our woes and of all our backwardness and ignorance today.'[24]

Not only were ruptures between African peoples a matter of practical concern for the leaders of the region, but they were also difficult to address. The character of tribalism in early 20th-century southern Africa was very much a product of the colonial encounter. Indeed, the authority and position of the intellectuals and traditional leaders gathered in Bloemfontein had the same ultimate causes as the tribalism that the ANC's founders abhorred.

Settlers brought with them to the continent a crude, essentialist conception of African ethnicity in which tribes were construed as timeless communities with distinct languages, cultures and physical features. In particular, whites viewed warrior tribes as inherently antagonistic and prone to bouts of internecine warfare. For their part, African leaders were more fully aware of the fluidity and historical complexity of their own societies and they understood that colonial powers had used tribal authorities as instruments of social control. Colonial administrators used chiefs to collect intelligence, maintain 'law and order', collect taxes, and extract labour. But when academics, missionaries and colonial anthropologists invented tribal practices and conjured pseudo-languages out of dialects, they also persuaded the new missionary-educated African elite to embrace many of these invented traditions.

Missionaries' teaching of written African languages developed the preconditions for modern tribalism by creating rigid linguistic divides within historically fluid language groups. Moreover, local chiefs and then-predominant clans participated in the creation of 'tribal' justifications for their power, in order to turn their own precarious and temporary hegemony into permanent rule. The chiefs and kings who bewailed imperial divide-and-rule strategy were at the same time among its principal beneficiaries.

The Christian-educated African elite likewise internalised the colonisers' interpretations of African history in the mission schools. They benefited from tribalism, serving as interpreters of tradition for the colonisers and as interpreters of colonial practice for the chiefs. As part of the educated native elite of the Empire, they were allowed a wide degree of political freedom and granted the opportunity to accumulate capital.

The emphasis of early ANC leaders on the unity of the African peoples of the region inevitably threw the spotlight onto quite different forms of division. Asserting the unity among the leaders of African societies brought into question the relationship between Africans and white settlers (and other racial minorities). In later decades, the affirmation of the unity of patriarchs raised the question of the participation of women in the authority structures of African society. For members of the Communist Party of South Africa (CPSA), ANC leaders' singleminded focus on the problem of ethnic division prevented them from grasping more fundamental sources of class division.

Non-racialism

After the SANNC's inaugural meeting in 1912, a committee was delegated the task of writing a constitution for the organisation. Among the central goals on which it agreed was the promotion of 'unity and mutual co-operation between the government and the South African Black people' and 'understanding between white and black South Africans'.[25] But African unity and cross-racial understanding would prove difficult for the movement's leaders to reconcile.

Despite the relatively small numbers of whites opposed to segregation, a measure of cross-racial collaboration was indeed a feature of the ANC from its inception. Non-racialism was primarily pioneered, however, by the CPSA. From the mid-1920s, the Party adopted a non-racial structure in which various races operated without differentiation within a single organisation. This principle was maintained despite the distinct political preoccupations of cadres of different races, with whites often focusing on electoral politics, for example, and blacks on labour agitation. The Party's theory of South Africa's colonialism of a special type (CST) placed bourgeois whites at the centre of a unique system of exploitation that exhibited the characteristics of both an imperialist state and a colony; but CST also emphasised the fundamental character of class, rather than racial, division.

White sympathisers with the ANC's struggle were often humanists drawn from the Protestant churches. The African educated elite that played such an important role in the ANC's early decades was inspired to adopt universalistic positions on political rights. As the international movement for universal human rights gained momentum towards the end of the Second World War, its influence was reflected in the ANC's 'African Claims' document, compiled in 1943 by an elitist committee of professional and religious leaders. This document was intended to appeal to African university graduates and to draw them into the movement. Its substance, however, included a clearly stated commitment to non-racial citizenship and a demand for a bill of rights embracing all South Africans.

At this point in its history, the ANC leadership had not yet recognised the full potential of cross-racial mass mobilisation. There was little consciousness within or outside the ANC about the precise meaning of labels such as 'multi-racial', 'interracial' and 'non-racial', which were used more or less interchangeably.[26] Moreover, the practical realisation of multi-racialism proved at times frustrating. The complex process of forging unity within racial groups – for example, between the Transvaal and Natal Indian Congresses or between black trade unions – inevitably re-emphasised the differences between racial groups.

The ANC persisted with a multi-racial logic in which separate racial congresses committed themselves to working together. In the decades ahead, it reiterated that separate race-based organisations should form the basic building blocks of a wider Congress Alliance. This Alliance was created when the ANC allied first with the South African Indian Congress (SAIC) in 1947 and then with the South African Coloured People's Organisation (SACPO) and the white South African Congress of Democrats (SACOD) in 1953. It was this full Congress Alliance that endorsed the Freedom Charter in 1956.

The retention of the Congress Alliance model reflected ambivalence about the relative merits of multi-racial and non-racial unity. There was concern in the ANC that whites and Indians, with their wealth and superior education, would be able to exert influence disproportionate to their numbers in a non-racial organisation. Such concerns were amplified by the presence of influential whites and Indians in the higher levels of the Communist Party, where alien Marxist ideas initially unappealing to Africanist intellectuals were vigorously propagated.

For such reasons, ANC leaders prohibited non-African membership and continued to insist that the overall Congress Alliance had an 'African-led' character. The ANC would retain an all-black membership until the Morogoro conference of 1969 and it retained an all-black leadership, at the national executive committee level, until 1985. Multi-racialism nevertheless failed to prevent whites and Indians, and particularly communists, from exercising precisely the disproportionate influence that Africanists feared. By virtue of their pre-caucusing and their representation on the coordinating structures of the Congress Alliance, they were probably able to exercise a power still more disproportionate to their numbers than their absorption into a non-racial mother body would have permitted.

Unity between races and ideologies created tensions that the ANC leadership struggled hard to contain. In 1958, the ANC president, Albert Luthuli, observed that 'we are not a homogeneous community, not as far as race and colour are concerned nor, possibly, even in culture ... I personally believe that here in South Africa, with all our diversities of colour and race, we will show the world a new pattern for democracy. What is important is that we can build a homogeneous South Africa on the basis not of colour but of human values.'[27] Multi-racial unity by means of the Congress

Alliance, and its ideological corollary of communist ideological influence, ultimately proved impossible to reconcile with the demands of racial unity among oppressed Africans. By the later 1950s, the tensions between these different conceptions of unity had grown unmanageable and the Pan Africanist Congress (PAC) broke away from the ANC.

What is more, once the decision was taken (against the wishes of Luthuli) to move towards an armed struggle, a new instrument was created to perpetuate multi-racial collaboration. Umkhonto weSizwe (MK), the joint armed wing of the ANC and the re-formed SACP, was a non-racial organisation. More importantly, the SACP was the dominant force in the leadership of MK, and through the armed wing the Party exerted a powerful indirect influence on the ANC.

The exile ANC adopted a two-pronged approach to the unity of the movement. The rallying calls of unity and discipline became instruments in the battle to bolster morale and avert fragmentation during difficult decades of political impotence. The value of unity was also deployed to support ANC diplomats' demands that it should serve as the sole legitimate representative of the oppressed people of South Africa in international forums. But political developments back in the country created enormous difficulties for the ANC's notion of unity. The Soweto uprising

Chief Albert Luthuli and Oliver Tambo, Johannesburg, 1959.
(Alf Kumalo)

© Drum Social Histories / Baileys African History Archive / Africa Media Online

generated international interest in apartheid and it precipitated an invitation for O.R. Tambo to address the General Assembly of the United Nations. However, as the ANC's official mouthpiece *Sechaba* observed, the emergence of a black consciousness movement within South Africa might allow 'the imperialists' to 'form an alternative to the ANC or to split our national liberation forces'.[28] Later developments, such as Nelson Mandela's negotiations with the regime while under detention in Pollsmoor prison, and the emergence of autonomous labour unions, were also viewed with great suspicion by ANC leaders on the grounds that they might divide the liberation movement into internal and exile wings, or otherwise propagate division and disharmony.

Unity in theory

In the present time, the ANC's pursuit of the principle of unity is no longer confined to the Congress system or to the spheres of race and ethnicity. The ANC has developed a complex system of alliances that allow diverse class, ideological, gender and generational differences to be expressed and yet at the same time remain incorporated into a wider project. The key instrument of cross-institutional unification today is the 'tripartite alliance' between the ANC, the Congress of South African Trade Unions (Cosatu) and the SACP. The SACP is a faction within the liberation movement that possesses an unusual degree of intellectual independence and influence. Cosatu must survive in a competitive labour environment which limits its leaders' ability to strike lasting deals with the ANC. The ANC also boasts women's and youth leagues which lobby around the concerns of particular constituencies while remaining constitutionally subservient to the mother body. All of these entities have become embroiled in recent factional contests for power and position within the ANC.

The ANC has also sought out accords and partnerships elsewhere in the political system. It has engaged in relationships of some depth and endurance with Africanist and black consciousness competitors, the Inkatha Freedom Party, and the New National Party. And it has adopted similar tactics in civil society, building relationships with traditional leaders, churches and NGOs. In such circumstances ANC leaders expect reciprocity of a special kind. Civil society partners can make representations to the ANC but at the same time they are expected to refrain from open denigration of the movement.

The ANC's capacity to maintain an appearance of unity and to consolidate such a wide array of alliances is sometimes explained in terms of African social conservatism and a preference for consensus over contestation. Nelson Mandela once celebrated the

Launch of Cosatu, Durban, 1985. (Paul Weinberg)

THE
RLD UNI

idealised democracy of tribal meetings that he observed in his childhood, in which the fundamental equality of men was expressed through a right and freedom to speak regardless of rank and social position. 'All men', Mandela claimed, 'were free to voice their opinions and were equal in their value as citizens.' Moreover, he added, 'majority rule' was a notion alien to such societies and 'a minority was not to be crushed by a majority'.[29]

The ANC has in recent decades conceptualised its project to achieve a more just society by using the language of 'national democratic revolution' (NDR). This pseudo-revolutionary conception of political transformation was introduced into the ANC's strategic documents in the 1960s by communist intellectuals who were trying to conceptualise the relationship between their overarching goal of international socialism and the immediate anti-colonial project of national liberation. Since the 1920s, the Communist Party has subordinated long-range socialist goals to the immediate struggle for national independence, and post-colonial liberation struggles were greeted in Moscow as broadly anti-imperialist and anti-Western. But the Party did not want national liberation to jeopardise the ultimate attainability of the second-stage transition to a socialist future.

The orthodox view of NDR is that it is 'a process of struggle that seeks the transfer of power to the people'. Its 'strategic objectives' in this 'current phase' include the creation of 'a non-racial, non-sexist, democratic and united South Africa [in which] all organs of the state are controlled by the people'.[30] The theory of NDR is not specific about time frames or about the strategic relationships between avowed immediate (national) and ultimate (international socialist) objectives. The fundamental ambiguity and flexibility of this framework has been essential to its survival in post-apartheid, and indeed post-Soviet, conditions. The conceptual apparatus of NDR has allowed ANC leaders to maintain their commitment to a vaguely defined and overarching transformative project that holds the ANC together. The nebulous phases and stages of NDR can meanwhile be manipulated in order to deflect conflict, by separating and then conflating principles with tactics and immediate goals with ultimate social outcomes.[31]

NDR also provides a vocabulary for political argumentation that accommodates diverse protagonists and culminates in indeterminate and sometimes indecipherable conclusions. The SACP uses NDR to reiterate the ultimately anti-capitalist character of the ANC's historical project. Yet ANC centrists use it to isolate and castigate leftists in the trade unions and civil society whose naive pursuit of socialism today is 'voluntarist', ignores 'objective reality', and pursues 'simplistic or naive anti-capitalist objectives' inappropriate to this phase. Those on the right of the movement have been able to construe the current period as legitimately market-oriented in character. The precise socialist orientation of NDR, they have observed, is a matter for prolonged philosophical deliberation, and should not be seen as possessing any practical import or policy relevance in current conditions. The utility of the NDR framework for ANC leaders has therefore been its capacity to justify essentially pragmatic compromises between ANC constituencies. A non-racial, non-sexist and democratic society can only be built by addressing the needs and interests of the poor, most of whom are African and female. At the same time, liberal constitutionalism, despite its incompatibility with the ultimate demands of the revolution, can be, and has been, justified as an essential instrument in the current stage of that revolution.

Unsustainable unity

Nelson Mandela once observed that 'the ANC has never been a political party ... the ANC is a coalition ... Some will support free enterprise, others socialism. Some are conservatives, others are liberals. We are united solely by our determination to oppose racial oppression. That is the only thing that unites us.'[32] Some post-apartheid decline in ANC cohesiveness is therefore not a real surprise.

The pursuit of unity has brought stability and compromise to the ANC in government, but primarily by circumventing fundamental differences of principle rather than confronting them. Concerns about the ethical character of a market economy, liberal constitutionalism, and the nature and significance of race and ethnicity have been mediated and re-mediated, but they cannot be said to have been resolved. Differences and disagreements have resurfaced and sometimes gained fresh resonance in changed political conditions.

Arguments about the moral desirability and practical viability of alternatives to 'neo-liberalism' have recently been resurgent. The emergence of East Asian developmental states and the recent crisis in the international economy have both revitalised proponents of state-centred capitalism. Unprecedented demand for resources generated by rapid economic development in the South, and especially in China, has contributed to the rise of an ideologically charged 'resource nationalism' in oil- and mineral-producing countries, including South Africa.

But far greater challenges to ANC unity have

been generated by changes in the class character of the liberation movement itself. The growth of black business power and the emergence of the black middle classes have introduced new sets of interests into the movement's internal politics. The rising business elite can be found across the nation, embedded in the provincial and regional structures of the ANC and benefiting from the commercial opportunities created by state spending. Politicised business is especially prominent in Gauteng, and the province's moneyed classes have spread their tentacles into poorer but more populous provinces. Cadres who were 'deployed' to business to remove them from ANC power struggles have returned to politics with large war chests. Cycles of money and power can be found across the movement and in almost every part of the state machine.

Unity has come under further strain as Cosatu and the SACP have both become embroiled in recent factional politics. The coherence of Cosatu is now itself under threat as industrial, manufacturing and mineworker unions decline as a consequence of de-industrialisation. The growth of state employment will soon propel public-sector unions towards majority membership of the federation. Though the South African Democratic Teachers' Union (Sadtu), the National Education, Health and Allied Workers' Union (Nehawu) and the South African Municipal Workers'

Union (Samwu) use a proletarian vocabulary, their members are part of the emerging middle class. Their relationship to state power places them increasingly at odds with trade union members organising at the front lines of the capitalist economy. The vast majority of the ANC's nominally million-strong membership remains poor.

Overlain across such class tensions are new generational strains. A growing proportion of the ANC's active membership has no direct experience of the struggle for liberation and therefore no ingrained respect for conventions of authority and seniority. Many older ANC leaders recognise that the invented tradition of reconciling diverse interests in the pursuit of national democratic revolution will probably not survive generational change and the fading of the morality of the struggle.

In recent times, debates about race appear to be escaping the conventions of ANC non-racialism. The notion that the ANC is the champion of black people in general but also of Africans in particular, while remaining non-racial in orientation, is understandably confusing for new generations of activists. The appropriate usage and significance of the terms African, black and Coloured have once again become the matter of high-profile internal disputation. The predicament of racial difference continues to preoccupy policy makers, since it appears to be impossible to deploy race-based programmes of redress and restitution without intensifying citizens' identification with apartheid's system of racial classification.

It remains conceivable that political mobilisation might occur around anti-white sentiment. Many whites have capitalised on their skills and other asset advantages to secure work in the high-wage knowledge economy and to benefit from an appreciating suburban property market. Apartheid has been partially privatised as a result of the growth of security estates, guarded shopping complexes and leisure centres, private hospitals, and fortress business parks. The failure of opposition political leaders to press upon white citizens their responsibility for the prolonged ramifications of apartheid leaves anti-white racial mobilisation as a potential instrument in the armoury of a future political populist.

The ANC has been right to insist that multi-racial or multi-national or multi-ethnic societies should not privilege one group over others except in pursuit of historical redress. This is far from being solely a South African problem. Most post-colonial states are more diverse than European societies in terms of language, religion, ethnicity and the presence of significant migrant populations. The challenge that post-colonial regimes confront is how to incorporate such diversity into political and governmental systems so that group identities can be expressed without compromising loyalty to national-level state institutions.[33]

The Indian National Congress (INC) is sometimes proposed as the custodian of a more successful organisational tradition. Early INC leaders celebrated the advantages of diversity and open political contestation during the first three decades of independence. They resisted the idea that a single movement should impose a homogeneous system of public authority upon a complex society, or a rigid disciplinary framework on a diverse congress movement. Patriotism was directed to the state rather than to the 'nation'. Institutional innovations were introduced to allow communities to enjoy a degree of cultural and religious self-determination – in particular, a form of 'asymmetric federalism' that conferred different powers upon different territorial units and a 1956 State Reorganisation Act that allowed constituent states to develop distinct ethnic or linguistic bases. Political leaders meanwhile largely shunned majoritarianism and encouraged 'centric-regional' parties that operate at both provincial and national levels simultaneously. Yet despite all these efforts, post-independence India has certainly not escaped violence and division. Today it is in the grip of yet another wave of communal violence, and the state is engaged in the violent suppression of widely dispersed and numerous quasi-Marxist 'Naxalite' rebellions.

Unity and oneness

The ANC has recently experienced unexpected political upheavals, which include the tumultuous election of a new leadership at the 2007 national conference in Polokwane. Conflict and factional struggle are widespread. In response, an anti-pluralist tendency has emerged in party documents dealing with legitimate lobbying for office. Disciplinary proceedings have been used to constrain outspoken youth leaders, and new legislation has been contemplated to control the public flow of information about the actions of public authorities. 'Profound cultural practice' supposedly prohibits self-promotion or canvassing, a prohibition on lobbying or campaigning that leaves the electoral process open to manipulation by the leadership. Such a drive for unity can preclude the idea of legitimate division. One recent correspondent to an ANC publication wrote as follows: 'No movement can endure the disorganization caused by disunity within its ranks ... History is littered with examples of how even the most popular revolutionary movements were crushed and defeated simply on the basis of divisions within their ranks.'[34]

Luthuli House, the ANC's headquarters, has been

impelled to contain factionalism, to neutralise ethnic and racial politics, to regulate careerism and to ensure respect for established policy positions. But this has been accomplished by means of a centralisation of control that has stifled debate, imposed favoured candidates and limited competition for office so relentlessly that a backlash on the part of branch activists and provincial structures became inevitable. Provincial counter-reactions against central control have been part of ANC politics since the interwar years. But today they possess a greater gravity because of the scale of rebellions and the capacity of organised factions at all levels of the party to build sizeable war chests from state funds.

In the state itself, there has been continued dissatisfaction among ANC leaders about the idea and practice of the separation of powers. A preference for ANC unity was spelled out in its 1994 Strategy and Tactics document: 'The ANC should ensure that the movement is not split into various sections – extra-parliamentary, parliamentary and executive or alternatively national, provincial and local – but [should] exercise its leadership function as one united movement acting together in pursuit of common goals regardless of where its members are deployed.'

The national parliament has repeatedly been subordinated to the party in the executive. As a result of the fused executive and legislature in South Africa's parliamentary system, the governing party needs to adopt a deliberate anti-centralising strategy if it is to build parliamentary oversight capacity. Instead, the ANC caucus code of conduct privileges party unity over parliamentary autonomy. The ANC has made it politically hazardous for parliamentarians to perform legislative and oversight functions.

The president of the country is elected by the National Assembly, and appoints a cabinet that is collectively responsible to parliament. Cabinet governs together with the president. Since the ANC's rise to government, power has drifted from society to state, from provincial to national level, from the legislature to the executive, and, within the national executive, from cabinet to presidency. A powerful presidency is to some extent a response to the challenges of service delivery and policy coordination. However, it can also provide a vehicle for personalised rule, it can be abused to exercise unaccountable power, and succession problems are likely to arise as factions compete for a prize that no significant political or economic actor dare leave in the hands of others.

As a result in part of the ANC's relative electoral popularity, the accountability of the executive to the legislature, and of government to the electorate, can both be circumscribed on grounds of respect for the will of the people. The negative impacts of electoral dominance of this kind tend to increase the longer they endure. An unbalanced party system endangers effective political opposition and weakens the boundaries between state and party. When a genuine electoral challenge finally emerges, a dominant party may be tempted to buy votes, abuse public authority, manipulate the electoral commission and stifle media freedoms.

The pursuit of unity can become a dangerous pathology. This phenomenon was analysed in early post-colonial Africa in Aristide Zolberg's elegant 1966 treatise, *Creating Political Order: The Party States of West Africa*. Zolberg observes that most African nations reached independence with a single nationalist movement laying claim to a near-monopoly of power, opposed only by a scattering of weak and regionalist opposition parties. Such party dominance often followed a common pattern. The nationalist party leadership stepped into the shoes of the departing colonial powers, and immediately donned their mantle of unquestioned authority. They spoke on behalf of 'the masses' as the privileged interpreters of a general will.

The colonial power usually bequeathed a fragmented society, because tribalism had been used as an instrument of division and control. For this

ANC election campaign, Cape Town, 1994. (Paul Grendon)

reason, nationalist elites recognised the importance of building a central authority to counter ethnic division. Rather than representing a healthy pluralism, however, the resultant managed tribalist divisions persisted and turned sour. The 'unity' that came from party-enforced unity was therefore shot through with political tensions and psycho-social strains.

Electoral success in founding elections then promoted party leaders to well-paid government positions and allowed them access to government budgets and the instruments of state patronage. Once these advantages became clear, other elites quickly gravitated to the ruling party to share in its power and command of public resources. The governing elite then expanded by incorporating the leaders of outsider ethnic groups. Such bandwagon effects were interspersed with episodes of fragmentation and confusion, as political entrepreneurs tried to use ethnic appeals or kinship relations to secure building blocks of support for use as negotiating chips in the struggle for resource access. Meanwhile, the assertion of the power of the dominant party was presented as an assertion of support for unity and away from unnatural colonial-inspired divisions.[35]

The post-colonial societies that Zolberg studied were all exceptionally complex in their linguistic and religious patterns. They all, moreover, covered large and hard-to-control territories over which alien colonial boundaries had been superimposed. Given that the colonial powers had created the evil division that marred social unity, the party could claim to be pursuing a moral project of unification. This inclusive project to build oneness by incorporation was presented as more authentically African than political competition and pluralism.

The most widely shared collective membership in such a society was membership of the party itself. Joining the party represented a commitment to a social contract and an assertion of personal commitment to assist in the creation of a moral community. Unity in such circumstances appeared to be an absence of opposition. Only those who were in some way morally defective would create or participate in political organisations that generated opposition or that divided instead of uniting.

In such circumstances, almost every social cleavage or difference could be defined as illegitimate. Classes, districts, tribes and religions could be portrayed as obstacles to unity. The people, party leaders began to assert, are one. The people act only through the party to build the new nation. For Zolberg, the party in such conditions can become 'the basis of the legitimacy of all other institutions. Ultimately it *is* the people, it *is* the nation. Therefore it must be one.'[36]

It is difficult to conceive of the emergence of such an anti-pluralist conception of moral unity in contemporary South Africa. But the pressures towards conformity and accommodation with the demands of the incumbent leadership have on occasion been very strong. Embattled leaders seeking justification for draconian controls on competition for office or on open political debate have sometimes constructed arguments for enforced discipline and censorship in the service of an imperative of unity. The 'democratic centralism' that the ANC has taken over from its SACP ally as an instrument of discipline echoes an idealised understanding of the governance of traditional African societies. According to this view, all members of the society have an opportunity to speak on matters of concern to them. The leadership must then consider the interests and values of the people and find a consensus that reflects and reaffirms an underlying societal unity.

Pluralism and competition, it must be said, are not 'natural' features of any political system. The partisan pursuit of narrow interests at the expense of communal cohesion and a wider purported 'public good' has been regarded as divisive across most of the political history of all societies, including the Western societies that today champion pluralism and political competition. 'Cabals', 'factions', 'cliques' and 'sects' have been castigated as injurious to the unity of the state, and as threats to the 'one perfect body' to which a Christian society should aspire. Only with the emergence of contract theories of the state in the late 17th century did the idea of irreducible and conflicting interests, bound by an overarching contract with one another, begin to gain any imaginative hold.

Pluralism is therefore a precarious attainment rather than a given political condition. Even where an open political order has been constitutionally entrenched, an embattled governing party can define party and factional differences as morally unacceptable and the pursuit of divergent interests as a threat to the 'national interest'. Patriotism can very quickly be turned into conformism; the legitimate jostling of interests can be portrayed as selfish opportunism. The ANC has not settled upon a philosophy of government that can reliably generate internal cohesion and social solidarity without threatening to incapacitate opposition or to suppress diversity and dissent.

4

Liberation

The African National Congress (ANC) is a registered political party that competes for election in a constitutional representative democracy. The movement's leadership steadily defends the constitutional order that was established in 1996 as the cornerstone of the country's political transition. ANC activists claim that the movement has taken a great step forward by liberating the South African people from the evil system of apartheid and introducing a democratic and constitutionalist order.

Yet the ANC also claims to be a liberation movement whose project to emancipate the people from oppression has not yet run its course. It remains dedicated to freeing the South African people from the chains of colonialism of a special type; it seeks to emancipate the citizens of post-apartheid society from the persistent false consciousness that has perpetuated sexism and racism; it aims to liberate South Africans

– together with the poor of the global South and, ultimately, all of the world's oppressed peoples – from the chains of global capitalist exploitation; and it is home to a range of redemptive and transcendental conceptions of human liberation. The unending struggle to free human beings from all forms of oppression and repression has left ANC intellectuals uncertain and divided about the value and significance of the achievement of representative democracy in 1994.

Dimensions of human freedom

The democratic elections of 1994 marked an incontestably important moment in the history of South Africa. The ANC had been formed in 1912 in reaction against the Act of Union. Resentment against white rule deepened thereafter as black subjects were progressively denied opportunities to purchase land, to accumulate capital and to participate in the commercial life of the country. In the era of high apartheid, their restrictions and disabilities were systematically extended and separate development assigned their identities and their citizenship to regime-sponsored Bantustans.

Much of the historical legacy of oppression was lifted by the 'democratic transition'. It brought with it a raft of political liberties and an entitlement to

Voter education on a farm outside Potchefstroom, 1994.
(David Goldblatt)

participate in the economic life of the society. But for many black citizens this political milestone could not be equated with liberation. All conceptions of what it is to be free share the underlying idea that our freedom is diminished when we are unable to realise our purposes. Liberal intellectual traditions, with which most white South Africans feel comfortable, understand liberty as an absence of external and personal constraints on human beings' ability to act as they please. On this view, we are unfree when the state fails to respect and protect a realm of individual liberty defined by our civil and political rights. And such rights include a right to enjoy the possession of private property. The key political institutions of liberal democracy that flow from such an understanding of freedom are those that protect individual rights to speak, vote, organise and accumulate. The threats to such freedom come not only from fellow citizens but also, and perhaps primarily, from the modern state itself.

In recent years the political settlement entrenched by the constitution of 1996 has come under fire. Some activists argue that the process of preparing the constitution was flawed in that the final agreement was shaped not by considerations of justice but by the symmetry of bald power between the principal negotiating parties. The beneficiaries of apartheid, on this view, used their unjustly acquired wealth and their residual control of the forces of coercion to secure a constitutional settlement that entrenched and reproduced their advantages across future generations. A related criticism that has recently been widely aired by the ANC Youth League is that the constitution reflects a settlement in the realm of (bourgeois) politics and does not address the need for economic justice and 'economic freedom'.

Many ANC veterans are not persuaded by the merits of liberal political ideas. Constraints on freedom, they observe, need not be external and personal, and so the mere protection of rights and liberties will not suffice to lift them. Even when black citizens are no longer denied political rights, their lack of assets and skills can leave them effectively in chains.

A desire to instil a richer conception of freedom into the post-apartheid political settlement was reflected in the incorporation of socio-economic rights into the constitution. Government is accordingly responsible not merely for protecting the liberties associated with a liberal democracy but also with progressively realising rights to shelter, health, education and other practical preconditions for a dignified life. The design of the final constitution of 1996 also embodied concerns about equality, dignity, and human solidarity. It was in this sense a product of the tradition of Christian liberalism that ran through the ANC from its formation, and that was expressed in the 'African Claims' document and the Freedom Charter.

All the same, liberation still cannot be enjoyed if the resources and capabilities required to realise positive rights cannot be accessed. For many ANC activists, such resources are rendered inaccessible by the fundamental structural characteristics of a market-based economy embedded in an international capitalist order.

The leftist orientation of the national democratic revolution has helped the left of the tripartite alliance to contest the emergence of a culture of elite enrichment in the ANC. Communist intellectuals introduced the NDR doctrine to the ANC four decades ago to avert the destruction of socialist ambitions and organised labour by rapacious nationalist elites – consequences they had witnessed in other post-colonial societies. While the SACP has been willing to accept necessary ideological compromises, such as bourgeois democracy and private property, it has been determined to prevent victorious nationalist or bourgeois elites from closing down a future road to socialism. The revolutionary timetable dictates that fiscal prudence and minimal redistribution are needed 'in the current phase' when international capitalism must still be accommodated, but actions that result in irreversible steps away from a socialist future must not be accepted.

The post-apartheid ANC ostensibly remains

dedicated to freeing the South African people from the chains of colonialism. The rebellion that culminated in the negotiated transition must by its nature remain incomplete because, as the theory of colonialism of a special type observes, the colonial power remains embedded within the borders of the society – and it is embedded in the economy and governance systems of the post-apartheid 'democracy'. Beyond the borders of the state, moreover, neo-colonial and imperialist forces continue to dominate the international order, and the movements of capital and power that they control can bring about an effective neo- or re-colonisation. Such sinister forces can be countered only by the solidarity of forces for liberation, even at the expense of limiting bourgeois political freedoms and subverting liberal institutions.

* * *

The ANC has also claimed that it is seeking to liberate the citizens of a post-apartheid representative democracy from the false consciousness that perpetuates sexism and racism. Inspired by a mix of liberal, feminist and black consciousness ideas, it has sought to achieve this second dimension of liberation by lifting the internalised psycho-social constraints on the self-realisation of black people and women.

Although the ANC condemned black consciousness doctrines in the 1970s for their lack of intellectual scope and rigour, many of the movement's later leaders were 'converts' drawn from BC backgrounds. The black consciousness tradition highlighted how inhibitions could be internalised by blacks under racial oppression and white supremacy. A consequent lack of self-belief, until redressed, must remain a powerful constraint on black people's ability to realise their purposes. Although the SACP viewed Steve Biko as an unwitting ally of pro-capitalist liberals, the ideas he propagated were reworked and strenuously advanced by ANC leaders, most notably Thabo Mbeki, in the 1980s and 1990s. Although it is difficult to make any reliable assessment of the intellectual legacy of black consciousness, many of the ideas promoted today by ANC activists, particularly among the youth, bear a BC imprint.

The liberation of women also occupies a prominent place in the ANC's contemporary rhetoric of national democratic revolution. The men who ran the early ANC were unwilling to extend full membership of the movement to women until 1943, until which time the ANC's Women's League had the reputation of being a 'catering auxiliary'.[37] Little attention was paid to the specific concerns of women and their participation in political activity was generally discouraged. Such exclusion is unsurprising in the light of the African elite's conception of gender roles in this period. Urbanised African men drew upon longstanding ideas that men were allowed to participate in a community's political affairs when they reached adulthood. Such a view overlapped with the understanding in British society of the political responsibilities of adult men. More generally, African men and women alike had been influenced by the gender division between public and private realms that they observed in the lives of middle-class European (primarily English) settler families.[38] The presumption that men were the primary participants in political life was tightly connected to a struggle over the denial of full adulthood to Africans, most notably when the franchise was denied to Africans.

Women's involvement in political struggle was nevertheless precipitated by the pass laws, which left black women vulnerable to victimisation by the police. In the 1940s and 1950s, there were rural uprisings against pass laws and boycotts of municipal beer halls with the aim of maintaining women's income from home brewing. In response to government attempts to extend and intensify pass controls on women in major urban centres in the 1950s, the political organisation of African women through the Women's League developed rapidly. Women's League leaders quickly

STOP HARASSING OUR MOTHER STOP

WINNIE NOMZAMO MANDELA

THE NATION SALUTES AND SUPPORTS
YOU AND ALL THOSE WHO OPPOSE
BOTHA'S UNJUST LAWS.
"THERE SHALL BE HOUSES, SECURITY, AND COMFORT"

ISSUED BY THE WINNIE MANDELA SUPPORT COMMITTEE IN
CONJUNCTION WITH THE RELEASE MANDELA COMMITTEE.
1st FLOOR PORTLAND PLACE, 37 JORISSEN STREET, BRAAMFONTEIN.

A woman protests against state harassment of Winnie Mandela, Johannesburg, 1986. (Gille de Vlieg) built partnerships with women's organisations in the trade union movements and elsewhere in civil society. The Federation of South African Women (Fedsaw) secured the right to participate in the drawing up and ratification of the Freedom Charter in 1955. The following year, around 20,000 women of all races converged on the Union Buildings to protest against the extension of pass laws.

All the same, the ANC leadership continued to accord priority to problems that could be analysed through the lenses of race and class. Women were virtually absent from the national executive committee until 1991. Despite the organisational and political weakness of the Women's League in recent years, the emancipation of women has continued to be addressed by means of appointment quotas. There has been a raft of legislation addressing unfair discrimination, employment equity, domestic violence and sexual offences since 1994. Women comprise half of ANC members of parliament and fill half of government portfolios. In 2007 the ANC national conference agreed that there should be gender parity in ANC structures.

But female quotas also place power in the hands of incumbent-dominated candidate and delegate list committees within the ANC. The wives and female relatives of power brokers have often been catapulted up candidate lists ahead of legitimate male challengers.

Moreover, the championing of an overarching project to create a non-racial and non-sexist South Africa helps incumbent leaders to rise above more immediate conflicts of ideology and interest within the movement. The pursuit of long-range goals under the auspices of the national democratic revolution enables senior leaders to deflect criticism of current policies on the grounds that they are appropriate to a particular phase of the struggle. Nevertheless, the anti-capitalist and consciousness-lifting aspects of the ANC's political project help to explain why the language of liberation continues to play a prominent part in conceptions of the ANC's historical project.

Christianity and liberation

The most prominent founders of the ANC were Christian converts educated in mission schools. Religious organisations became proving grounds for prominent figures across the history of the struggle. Together with the trade unions, churches were the principal vehicles through which black political activists could build skills and access resources. Churches provided opportunities for Africans to develop managerial capacities, to travel and to build national and international networks. After opposition political parties were banned in 1960, churches became sites of protest and deliberation and centres of political refuge and moral support. The local variants of liberation theology that emerged in the late 1960s helped to shape the black consciousness ideology that mobilised educated youth in the 1970s.

Even today, the ANC leadership continues to maintain links with religious organisations and to target its election campaigns at religious congregations. President Jacob Zuma famously observed in 2009 that the ANC is 'blessed in heaven' and that it will 'rule until Jesus comes back'. ANC members, he remarked somewhat light-heartedly, are on a 'fast track to heaven', whereas opposition voters support 'the man who carries a fork' and 'cooks people'.

Christians and communists in the ANC have shared a long-range view of historical change and a preoccupation with the role of extra-historical agency and inevitability in human affairs. The compatibility in practice between certain Christian and socialist conceptions of ANC strategy was made possible by the character of Christian belief in the early decades of the last century. The early Christian converts, as we have seen, were post-millennial in orientation and they believed in the inevitability of human social improvement. They possessed a conception of the millennium: a non-racial society in which the status of each individual is determined by his or her personal character and actions rather than by race.

Women dancing in Xhosa dress, Cosatu women's conference, Durban, 1988. (Santu Mofokeng)

Almost all such believers have nevertheless been discouraged by their religion from celebrating the disorder and conflict intrinsic to liberal representative democracy. Healthy democratic competition in a pluralist society can be interpreted by churchmen as the partisan pursuit of sectional interests and values at the expense of communal cohesion. Indeed, party politics have been regarded in just this way – as a divisive problem – across most of the political history of Christian societies. Cabals, factions and political parties themselves have been viewed as threats to the 'one perfect body' to which a Christian people should aspire. This view has echoed and reinforced African conceptions of the legitimacy of 'communal' governance. It is a small step from the celebration of one indivisible community to the demonising of the official opposition's leader as a promoter of unnecessary disunity.

In any event, the pre-millennial eschatology that informed most of the African independent churches precluded involvement in good works and social development. For the adherents of independent and Pentecostal churches, history has a pessimistic cast, and participation in earthly political affairs is viewed as a distraction from the demands of spiritual health. Change to this world will come not as a result of gradual historical improvement but rather from outside history with the return of the Kingdom of God, but only after the existing social order is destroyed in a cataclysmic process that will culminate in Armageddon.[39]

As the ANC moved closer to Communist Party collaborators and infiltrators in the 1920s and more profoundly in the early 1950s, the commonalities between socialist and New Testament conceptions of justice helped to accommodate the evident philosophical differences between them. The Christian values expressed in Acts 4, for example, have an appeal to socialists, whether scientific or utopian: 'There was no poor person among them, since whoever possessed fields or houses sold them ... and a distribution was made to each one in accordance with his needs.'

It may well be that conceptions of social justice have simultaneously changed both in the ANC and in many of the churches. Recent growth of organised religion in South Africa has been driven by the expansion of Pentecostal and related charismatic movements. Unlike Anglicans (who do not seem to believe that God plays very much role in everyday life), renewalists and Pentecostals believe that the Holy Spirit plays a direct and continuous role in everyday affairs. Many Pentecostals also believe that God will return to earth in their lifetime and their church doctrine is therefore preoccupied with the ends of history.

Women's prayer meeting, 1976. (David Goldblatt)

Many fast-expanding churches form part of the new 'prosperity theology'. A study by Pew Forum suggests that four out of every five South African Christians believe that God 'grants material prosperity to all believers who have enough faith'.[40] In many fast-growing churches, white and black, worshippers are preoccupied with the blessings to which they feel entitled as a result of their faith. Church services include testimonials that link religious devotion to wealth. The pastors who lead these churches demand substantial tithes and enjoy lavish personal lifestyles. The plight of the poor must not be ignored, they preach, but personal wealth should nevertheless be celebrated and pursued. In the words of the Rhema Church's school of business, believers should also aspire to 'impact the marketplace with Christ'.

There are some remarkable ethical parallels between these prosperity churches and the contemporary liberation movement. In a prosperity church, worshippers' tithes support the ostentatious wealth of the pastor, and the congregation's members understand their success and bodily health as signs of divine intervention and as rewards for their religious devotion. In the contemporary ANC, wealthy cadres make substantial donations to support the administrative and campaigning expenses of the movement. When they do business, they give the ANC a cut of the spoils. The tenders and job opportunities that come their way are accepted as an expression of grace – as a sign that they are in good standing with the movement to which they have devoted their lives.

It is probably the questionable legitimacy of new-found wealth that explains these striking parallels. The ANC and the new churches have not forgotten the poor, but they do not know how to help them. Yet it remains an affront against African communalist ethics – and, indeed, against the morality of any decent society – for individuals to live in luxury amidst a sea of poverty, while withholding the fruits of their good fortune from their extended families and communities. The ANC and the prosperity churches have found a way to render such personal enjoyment of wealth legitimate in a morally intricate but profoundly unequal society.

Marxism and liberation

The SACP has imported Marxist theory into the doctrines and programmes of the ANC. It has also brought with it many of the intellectual paradoxes and moral limitations of international communism. Across the history of Marxism, there has been an apparent paradox in its approach to morality.[41] Marx's avowed followers have claimed that systems of morality are essentially illusions that serve class interests. Moral ideas, like other systems of concepts, grow out of a particular mode of production and serve the interests of the dominant classes of that mode. The ideas prevalent in capitalist society help to justify the inequality, oppression and injustice of a political and economic system that dehumanises and exploits human beings. Marxists also use this same mode of analysis to explain the emergence and attractiveness of religious doctrines. The writings of Lenin, in particular, attack the 'falseness of all fables about morality'. Morality must be relentlessly unmasked and condemned as an anachronism.[42]

At the same time, Marxists are among the planet's most vehement and relentless moralisers. They are fierce critics of poor working conditions, worker exploitation, servitude and slavery. Condemnation, exhortation and exaggerated moral outrage are the staples of socialist and communist sloganeering. It is in this spirit that the ANC remains committed to the freeing of South Africans, the peoples of the global South and, ultimately, all the world's oppressed peoples, from the evil chains of global capitalist exploitation.

The apparent paradox between Marxism's simultaneous dismissal and embrace of moral condemnation can be explained by the long-range and future-oriented character of the morality of Marxism. In today's capitalist society, the prevalent moral ideas – such as political rights – are absurd bourgeois constructs that protect the expropriating classes. But it is nevertheless possible to make moral judgements that, for Marxists, have a sound intellectual foundation. Marxists are 'consequentialists' – they judge the moral character of actions in the light of their consequences. Good and bad actions can be differentiated on the basis of their implications for the ultimate attainment of emancipation from capitalism and from the wage slavery and alienation associated with it.

For Marx, revolution will set people free from a history of human bondage that culminated in wage slavery and exploitation. After the socialist revolution, a social order will arise in which human beings will be able to realise their potential and true nature. In capitalist society, the right of man to liberty is the right to be separate and so the right to be a restricted individual. The right to property is a right to a fundamentally inhuman self-interest. Marxists have seen emancipation as consisting not merely in an escape from the consequences of class society (self-interest, separateness), but also in freedom from the conditions that bring about such separation and alienation. Revolutionary politics are therefore the pursuit of emancipation from the bourgeois 'rights' to separation and to personal consumption, and from the capitalist conditions that call into being such individual rights. Marxists cannot accord respect to 'bourgeois

Hostel leaders discuss the petrol-bombing of their offices, Nyanga, Cape Town, 1987. (Chris Ledochowski)

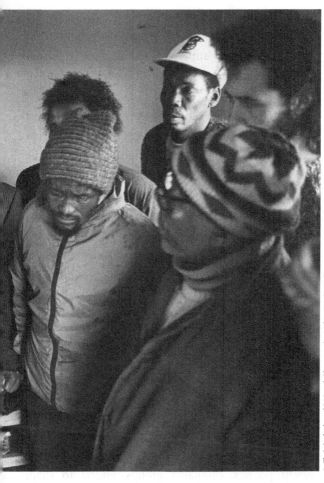

freedoms', because they are not really freedoms at all. Such rights and associated liberal institutions form part of the political 'superstructure' of capitalism from which human beings must be liberated by means of revolution.

Some liberation movement intellectuals, most notably the SACP deputy general secretary Jeremy Cronin, have claimed that bourgeois rights can be borrowed from the ANC's Christian liberal traditions and appended to the moral doctrines of the SACP. But the moral authority of the revolutionary conception of liberation must ultimately conflict with respect for liberal institutions and political rights. In the face of grinding poverty and entrenched historical disadvantage, political liberty – and its guarantors in representative democracy and the rule of law – must come to seem at best minimal and impoverished achievements. For consistent Marxists they are diversions from the project of human emancipation.

For their part, ANC leaders have found it difficult to treat parliamentary and judicial institutions with the respect that liberal constitutionalism demands. The movement has also balked at pluralist pressure-group politics, campaign groups' efforts to shape public policy, and the open competition of interests and ideas that is central to liberal conceptions of freedom. The 'bourgeois democracy' of rights, parliaments and constitutions is only a provisional accomplishment at best; and many ANC intellectuals demand a participatory democracy in which the mobilised masses directly drive transformation.

Party veterans are sometimes less concerned with whether important decisions are actually taken by the citizenry than with whether those decisions advance what the ANC understands as the 'real interests' of the people. The false moral consciousness generated by the capitalist mode of production means that ordinary people must be guided about right and wrong by the scientific analysis of the party elite. And the elite is committed to making long-range and consequentialist judgements based on how actions and events contribute to the realisation of a necessarily somewhat hazily defined emancipation.

It is for these reasons that the real testing of ANC activists' commitment to liberal institutions will come only when the ruling party finally faces a genuine electoral challenge. At this point, a conflict will arise between the demands of the bourgeois system of liberal rights and institutions and the longer-term consequences of electoral defeat for the prospects of human liberation. A moral obligation to obstruct free campaign activity, stifle media independence and curtail political freedoms will then presumably arise for SACP and ANC leaders who have sincerely adopted a liberationist world-view. In such circumstances, the wider lack of genuine enthusiasm for liberal democratic ideas and institutions in the ANC, instilled across generations of revolutionary equivocation, could prove liberal democracy's undoing.

5

Conclusion

The ANC has prevailed, or at least survived; but can it govern? The struggle against apartheid allowed questions about the ultimate character and purposes of the liberation movement to be deflected. It created solidarity and helped leaders to leave the character of human emancipation undefined. What purposes should the ANC serve, now that its immediate goal of overturning the apartheid regime has been accomplished?

One enduring feature of ANC intellectual life has been self-consciousness. The ANC is a mechanism of deliberation and reflection; and its favourite object of contemplation is itself. Cadres ruminate about the ANC's history, character, leadership and destiny. They lovingly detail the movement's foundation and early structures; the 'African Claims' document adopted in 1943; the 1949 Youth Congress putsch; the 'coordinating structures' and 'joint action councils' of the Congress Alliance; the M-Plan; the 'turn to armed struggle'; Morogoro; the Revolutionary Council and the 'politico-military councils'; the 'four pillars' of the struggle; Kabwe; the 'strategic centre of power'; and so, sometimes interminably, on and on.

In this introverted historical drama, external events and processes play drop-in roles, giving context to strategic shifts, changing doctrines, organisational reforms and conference resolutions. For some ANC intellectuals, the extraordinary history of 20th-century South Africa has served primarily as a backdrop for the narrative that really matters: the endless internal organisational and ideological renewal of the liberation movement itself.

Indulgent self-consciousness is better than no self-consciousness at all, of course, and ANC intellectuals have anyhow proved capable of episodes of searing self-criticism. Leaders have looked after themselves very well since 1994 – but they have also berated themselves for doing so. The trade unions and communists have been condemned for obstructionism but also praised for pulling the movement back repeatedly, but not too energetically, to a properly leftist historical orientation. 'A capacity for introspection, self-criticism and grasping the nettle of corrective action, when necessary', as one ANC intellectual observes, has 'ensured that the ANC remained relevant while other movements dithered, then withered.'[43] Because the ANC is a voluntary mass political movement, and reflects the poor, partly corrupt and unequal society in which it operates, its leaders need to exhibit a high degree of self-reflection if they are to realise benevolent government or even to survive.

The movement institutionalises self-assessment by means of its formal organisational and political reports and its 'strategy and tactics' documents. Some of its leaders have described the ANC as possessing a 'rational centre' – an enticing notion, perhaps at least partly descended from Leninist doctrines about the Party or from an idealisation of the deliberative character of African political life.

The factions that compete for offices and for economic opportunities in national and provincial politics are on most occasions not 'hard'. Activists nominated for one 'slate' of candidates are acceptable to the advocates of others, and some cadres will usually step back from the factionalist brink to support compromise. Policy and ideology are endlessly debated, so that although the ANC takes a lot of questionable decisions, it does so through a process that defers to the ideal of reason.

Now, however, consensus is threatened by changes in class structure and by the unequal political and economic opportunities these afford. Conflicts around race, ethnicity, patriarchy and the role of the young have surfaced or resurfaced. Reflecting endlessly on the past and parcelling out public resources to power brokers may temporarily hold the ANC together, but such actions also make it impossible to govern effectively. The ANC lacks any way to reconcile its purported destiny with the need to manage a contemporary capitalist state.

South Africans are far from irrevocably committed to the modern. In the early decades of the ANC's existence, traditional leaders such as chiefs and kings played a very significant role in the politics of the movement. Although the era of separate development and retribalisation undermined the moral authority of such leaders, it enhanced their control of some of the levers of resource distribution across rural society. The political resurgence of these leaders in the past decade is therefore not entirely surprising. Democratic competition has further exposed this social fault line, with campaigners for Jacob Zuma's election and re-election to the ANC presidency courting tribalists, traditional leaders, religious conservatives and homophobes – anyone in this conservative society who can be persuaded that Zuma is on their side – as well as embracing the more widely shared strategy of promising material rewards to potential supporters.

One way to understand the enduring appeal of tradition is through the Marxist concept of 'alienation'.

The failure of Marx's project to uncover the 'laws of motion' of capitalist society has done nothing to undermine the appeal of his analysis of the human condition under capitalist modernity. Labour under capitalism stunts man's intrinsic nature as a creative being, serves external rather than human needs, creates an obsessive need for money, and generates inhuman and unnatural desires. The potential of human beings is stifled, life is robbed of significant content, and communal reciprocity is destroyed. Ordinary people can neither control nor even understand the world in which they live.

Capitalism in South Africa has, relatively recently, brought about the destruction of pastoral societies organised around livestock and the land. It has been violent and tumultuous, and it has reproduced in a hundred million lives each and every negative facet of Marxian dehumanisation. This traumatic alienation has been intensified by the rapid imposition of European conceptions of skill and scientific knowledge, bureaucratic hierarchies and dehumanising modes of work organisation, all of which have been conceived as aspects of a racial supremacist project. Resistance against colonialism and apartheid has always been in part a struggle to secure some space for Africans to define their own values and identities in the face of such crushing processes of race-mediated alienation.[44]

South African communists and those influenced by them have nevertheless remained proponents of modernisation. For Marx, the capitalist epoch is a progressive phase in human history, because its productive dynamism creates the conditions for the transcendence of scarcity. Although Marx did not believe that it is possible to comprehend in advance the character of a communist society, it would represent a return to a world without alienation. History, on this (exceedingly optimistic) reading, is linear, but it is also a circle: that which matters, and which has been lost, shall be regained.

The second broad intellectual tradition within the ANC elite, built upon Christian missionary foundations, has enjoyed an easier relationship with modernity. On a sceptical reading, modernising petty bourgeois elites have been more than simply sensitive judges of the requirements of a capitalist economy. Many of the ANC's leading families have been driven by their pursuit of wealth and status (notwithstanding the Communist Party's strenuous efforts to layer socialist aims on top of this more fundamental goal). The organisation was formed by land-acquisitive chiefs and by the sympathisers of global commerce and Empire. Despite its efforts to organise the urban masses in the 1950s and early 1960s – with the assistance of the Communist Party and very much from above – the

ANC elite settled easily into the role of self-justifying military exile bureaucracy. It was scarcely a mobilising force in the 1980s but instead remained a detached elite dedicated to controlling or cannibalising the actual 'mobilising forces' of history.

Once in government, under a leadership representative of the rising commercial elite, the ANC used the theory of national democratic revolution to marginalise the left by deferring socialist ambitions to an imaginary future. This cleared the way for a more or less untrammelled pursuit of wealth, the manipulation of party institutions by business elites, the promotion of a political variant of prosperity theology, and a more generalised culture of elite enrichment.

Taken singly, and viewed in such an unforgiving light over their entire historical trajectories, the communist and Christian elite traditions are not especially edifying, intellectually or morally. But they have both been unequivocally modernising projects, insisting that the price that must be paid for modernity (largely, of course, by the little people) is well worth paying. And the two intellectual streams, always intermingled, were melded together by a self-conscious ANC leadership into a sustained project that more or less cohered – at least for a while.

Changes in the society's class structure (many of them driven by the ANC's own policies), the gradual erosion of crucial state capabilities, and the turbulence of the current international economy are unravelling the conditions for continued ANC unity. If the ANC is to survive – and there are no signs of any other party or movement on the horizon capable of managing this troubled society – it will need to do more than reassert the contradictory dogmas of the past.

This is not an especially good moment in human history to pursue emancipation from international capitalism. (Is it ever?) When secretary-general Gwede Mantashe recently pondered the longer-term purposes of the ANC, now that the apartheid regime is gone, he pointed to the enduring egalitarian and welfare state accomplishments of Swedish social democracy. This is an important intuition.

Over the course of the 20th century, communist ideas from the Soviet theoretical tradition exercised a growing influence on the ANC. In the 1930s and 1940s the movement had languished under a defensive Christian leadership, while the Communist Party organised boycotts, strikes and land invasions. After the Congress Youth instigated its putsch at the ANC's 1949 conference, the movement adopted such tactics as its own. In general, Marxism provided activists with a framework to comprehend the inexorable economic factors behind social and economic change. After the dissolution of the Comintern in 1943, however,

Soviet intellectuals and their Eastern European proxies fed South African Party intellectuals with doctrines that deepened and vulgarised their anti-capitalist sentiments. The 'capitalist state' was conceptualised crudely as a facilitator of capital accumulation, a coordinator of exploitation and an 'iron fist' of the appropriating class. Such dramatically negative conceptions of capitalist accumulation, and of the modern state, were understandably appealing in the era of high apartheid; but in our time they have formed a barrier to constructive post-apartheid government.

As we have seen, the ANC was denied by history the opportunity to engage with the international social democratic experience. Post-war social democracy partly humanised the capitalist economic system, as leftist parties built democratic, corporatist and welfare states that improved the lives of workers. They discovered the potential, but also the limitations, of nationalisation, collectivism, worker participation and new forms of international cooperation.

Today, ANC modernist aspirations are directed towards a 'developmental state' in deference to the economic achievements of post-war East Asia. Social democrats are surely right to insist, however, that a successful programme for economic development must be accompanied by a deep commitment to political liberty and to constitutionalism. The ANC itself needs liberal institutions to survive. Without an active press, effective courts and legislatures, functioning oversight bodies, nonpartisan checks on the abuse of political power and a strong opposition, it will very quickly destroy itself. Moreover, if the ANC succeeds in creating a more capable 'developmental' state, it will also need to develop a correspondingly more accountable one, in which the hazards of vertical subjugation – of citizens by the state itself – are fully recognised and more effectively neutralised.

The government's recently inaugurated National Development Plan offers a modest practical route map to a broadly social democratic future. The fashionable oxymoron of the 'democratic developmental state' also represents a belated attempt by ANC modernisers to address this lacuna. Yet ANC activists still seem unexcited – and sometimes actively repulsed – by such programmes for harnessing the dynamic energies of a capitalist economy while mitigating the inequality and alienation that such an economy generates.

At its formation, the ANC was committed to 'civilisation', to commerce and to what in later decades would become known as development. Is it possible that an antipathy towards 'Westernisation' – or perhaps an ambivalence about modernity itself – might persuade ANC activists to turn away from this legacy?

Social democracy and the developmental state

cannot serve as blueprints, because they emerged in quite different historical circumstances from those which prevail in South Africa today. They nevertheless suggest that a new and unifying strategic purpose can be created, and they contain clues about how economic development and a more equal society can be realised together. Each of these projects promises, however, a deepening of human alienation rather than its transcendence. A 'more dynamic' economy and a 'more capable' state demand an intensification of the authority of scientific and technological knowledge, a Weberian public sector bureaucracy, reorganised patterns of authority in the workplace, and the relentless advance of atomisation, marketisation and consumption.

Capitalist modernity has many faces and it continues to possess many attractions (particularly, for the new ANC elite, in the field of consumer goods). The modernity of state capitalist China has recently been touted within the ANC as promising the gifts of development (shopping and medicine) without the drawbacks of Westernisation. But the ANC cannot unequivocally champion even this culturally correct, anti-colonial conception of the modern. In the past decade, there has been a resurgence of interest within the ANC in authenticity, the recovery of African culture and the restoration of tradition, including a revisiting of the legitimate authority of traditional leaders. This does not mean that modernity is being rejected; but it does suggest that across society, and within the ANC itself, it is being selectively and only cautiously appropriated.

For these reasons it is essential that ANC leaders muster the intellectual and organisational energies required to launch a fresh post-apartheid project of emancipation through modernisation. If the leadership permits ambivalence about modernity to entrench itself further in the heart of the movement, political entrepreneurs will soon summon up empty fantasies about the land and about tradition. The stalled project of liberation through modernity may then become supplanted by a vain search for liberation from it.

Notes

1 African National Congress, 'Statement of the National Executive Committee of the ANC on the Occasion of the 100th Anniversary of the ANC' (Johannesburg, 2012).

2 African National Congress, 'Statement of the National Executive Committee', 1.

3 Moeletsi Mbeki, *Architects of Poverty* (London, Pan Macmillan, 2009), 6.

4 Wallace G. Mills, 'Millennial Christianity, British imperialism and African nationalism', in R. Elphick and R. Davenport (eds.), *Christianity in South Africa* (Cape Town, David Philip, 1997), 337–46.

5 Hlonipha Mokoena, *Magema Fuze: The Making of a Kholwa Intellectual* (Scottsville, University of KwaZulu-Natal Press, 2011).

6 Saul Dubow, *The African National Congress* (Johannesburg, Jonathan Ball, 2000), 13.

7 Dubow, *The ANC*, 34.

8 Jeremy Cronin, 'How should communists mark the ANC centenary?' *The Thinker*, 35 (2012), 20.

9 Tom Lodge, *Sharpeville: An Apartheid Massacre and Its Consequences* (Oxford, Oxford University Press, 2011), 180–6.

10 Lodge, *Sharpeville*, 232.

11 Vladimir Shubin, *ANC: A View from Moscow*, 2nd edition (Johannesburg, Jacana, 2008), 5.

12 Dubow, *The ANC*, 70–1.

13 Shubin, *ANC*, 66.

14 Hugh Macmillan, 'The Hani memorandum introduced and annotated', *Transformation* 69 (2009), 106–29.

15 Ivan Pillay, Interview with Howard Barrell, Lusaka, July 1989. Mayibuye Centre, University of the Western Cape.

16 See, for example, Raymond Suttner, *The ANC Underground in South Africa* (Johannesburg, Jacana, 2008).

17 Helena Pohlandt-McCormick, '"I saw a nightmare …" Doing violence to memory: The Soweto uprisings, June 16, 1976.' PhD thesis, Minnesota University, 1999.

18 Jacob Zuma, Interview with Howard Barrell, Lusaka, August 1989, sections 5 and 8. Mayibuye Centre, University of the Western Cape.

19 Shubin, *ANC*, 179, 257.

20 Dubow, *The ANC*, 91.

21 G.A. Cohen, *History, Labour and Freedom: Themes from Marx* (Oxford, Clarendon Press, 1988), 51–81.

22 Howard Barrell, 'Conscript to their age: African National Congress operational strategy, 1976–1986.' PhD thesis, Oxford University. [Available online] http://www.sahistory.org.za/archive/conscript-their-age-african-

national-congress-operational-strategy-1976-1986-howard-barrel-0 [accessed 28 August 2012].

23 Kgalema Motlanthe, 'Address to an ANC Youth League rally held at Nkowankowa, Limpopo', *ANC Today*, 12, 12 (2012).

24 Pixley ka Isaka Seme, 'Native Union' [24 October 1911], in T. Karis and G.M. Carter, *From Protest to Challenge, Volume 1: Protest and Hope, 1882–1934* (Stanford, Hoover Institution Press, 1972), 72.

25 Jacob Zuma, 'ANC centenary lecture: The legacy of President-General Pixley ka Isaka Seme', *ANC Today*, 12, 20 (2012).

26 David Everatt, *The Origins of Non-racialism in South Africa* (Johannesburg, Wits University Press, 2009), 4.

27 Albert Luthuli, 'Our vision is a democratic society'. Speech at a public meeting organised by the South African Congress of Democrats, 1 February 1958.

28 *Sechaba*, 13, 1 (1979), 1.

29 Andrew Nash, 'Mandela's democracy', *Monthly Review*, 50, 11 (1999).

30 Joel Netshitenzhe, 'The National Democratic Revolution and class struggle.' An address to the national executive committee of Cosatu. *The Shop Steward*, 9, 1 (2000), Section 1.

31 Netshitenzhe, 'National Democratic Revolution', Section 3.

32 Nelson Mandela, Interview with the *Washington Post*, 26 June 1990.

33 Alfred Stepan, Juan J. Linz and Yogendra Yadav,

Crafting State-Nations: India and Other Multinational Democracies (Baltimore, Johns Hopkins University Press, 2011).

34 Lazola Ndamase, 'Unity is strength', *ANC Today*, 12, 2 (2012), 20 January.

35 Aristide R. Zolberg, *Creating Political Order: The Party States of West Africa* (Chicago, Rand McNally, 1966), 21–35.

36 Zolberg, *Creating Political Order*, 47.

37 Natasha Erlank, 'Gender and masculinity in South African nationalist discourse, 1912–1950', *Feminist Studies* 29, 3 (2003), 653–72.

38 Erlank, 'Gender and masculinity', 660.

39 Mills, 'Millennial Christianity, British imperialism and African nationalism', 337–46.

40 Pew Forum, *Spirit and Power: A 10-Country Survey of Pentecostals* (Washington, Pew Forum on Religion and Public Life, 2006).

41 Steven Lukes, *Marxism and Morality* (Oxford, Oxford University Press, 1985).

42 Lukes, *Marxism and Morality*, 3–4.

43 Pallo Jordan, 'ANC: On a century of movement', *Mail & Guardian*, 23 December 2011.

44 Karl von Holdt, 'The South African post-apartheid bureaucracy', in Omano Edigheji (ed.), *Constructing a Democratic Developmental State in South Africa* (Cape Town, Human Sciences Research Council Press, 2010), 241–60.

Index